W9-DCU-792

MISSISSIPPI HARMONY

MISSISSIPPI HARMONY

Memoirs of a Freedom Fighter

WINSON HUDSON AND
CONSTANCE CURRY

Foreword by DERRICK BELL

MISSISSIPPI HARMONY

First published 2002 by
PALGRAVE MACMILLAN™
175 Fifth Avenue, New York, N.Y. 10010 and
Houndmills, Basingstoke, Hampshire, England RG21 6XS.
Companies and representatives throughout the world.

PALGRAVE MACMILLAN is the global academic imprint of the Palgrave Macmillan
division of St. Martin's Press, LLC and of Palgrave Macmillan Ltd. Macmillan® is a registered trademark in the United States, United Kingdom and other countries. Palgrave is a registered trademark in the European Union and other countries.

ISBN 0-312-29553-7 hardback

Library of Congress Cataloging-in-Publication Data
Hudson, Winson, 1916-
Mississippi Harmony : memoirs of a freedom fighter / by Winson Hudson, Constance Curry.
p. cm.
ISBN 0-312-29553-7
1. Hudson, Winson, 1916- 2. African American women civil rights workers—Mississippi—Biography. 3. Civil rights workers—Mississippi—Biography. 4. African Americans—Civil rights—Mississippi—History—20th century. 5. African Americans—Segregation—Mississippi—History—20th century. 6. Mississippi—Race relations. 7. Civil rights movements—Mississippi—History—20th century. 8. School integration—Mississippi—Leake County—History—20th century. 9. Leake County (Miss.)—Race relations. 10. Leake County (Miss.)—Biography. I. Curry, Constance, 1933- II. Title.

F350.N4 H83 2002
323.1'1960730762653'092—dc21

[B]
2002025843

A catalogue record for this book is available from the British Library.

Design by Letra Libre, Inc.

First edition: November 2002
10 9 8 7 6 5 4 3 2 1

Printed in the United States of America.

Winson Hudson dedicates this book to her daughter, Annie Maude Horton, and her grandsons, Donovan and Kempton Horton, who will carry on the struggle for freedom.

Constance Curry dedicates this book to her nephews, Walker and Coran Hendry, who will continue the work for peace and justice.

Oh come my dear children and sit by my knee,
And let me tell you the cost to be free.
If I don't tell you, you never will know,
Where you came from and where you should go.
You contributed more than any race in this nation,
Coming through hard trials and tribulation,
Fought in every war in America's name,
You never have dragged her flag to shame.
You see I'm swiftly passing away,
You can't afford to wait another day.
If I don't tell you, you never will know,
Where you came from and where you should go.

—*Winson Hudson, 1989*

CONTENTS

ACKNOWLEDGMENTS

There are many people who have worked long and hard to make this book a reality. We begin with those both of us need to thank. First, Winson's immediate family, Annie Maude Horton, Kempton and Lisa Horton, and Donovan and Dionne Horton have supported her on a daily basis from the very beginning. Her other relatives in Harmony, Joan Griffin, Annie Jean Hewitt, Addie Lou Hudson, Allean Leflore, Johnnie Gates Johnson, and Johnnie Bell McKee, have found information for us and have been willing to do whatever necessary to hasten the completion of the book. The same holds true for her relatives outside of Mississippi, Jewell Dassance, Cheryl G. Jones, Yvonne King, Angelean Mabry, and Anita Taylor. Jewell is the person who, along with Winson, encouraged me to write the book in the first place.

Winson's numerous friends and supporters in Leake County stood by to tell me more stories about Harmony and to do everything from read Winson copies of the manuscript, to tracking down Harmony acres on a county map, to wheeling her chair through the casino we visited. They are Pamela J. Carson, Mary Gates, Ruby Graham, Hazel Harvey, Karen Hunt, A. J. Lewis, Willie Earl Lewis, L. V. Overstreet, Richard Polk, Shirley Robinson, Claudette Rushing, Ferr Smith, Milton and Kathy Smith, and Bennie Thompson.

Winson's attorney and friend, Constance Slaughter Harvey, of Forest, Mississippi, and her physician and friend, Dr. Robert

Smith, of Jackson preserved her interests and her health. Frank Schwelb gave us great memories of his times in Harmony in the sixties, as did Derrick Bell, and Mel Leventhal. Marian Wright Edelman, Vernon Jordan, Joyce Miller, and Mary Norris have given Winson their friendship and support over many years.

The writers, scholars, and friends who recognized the value of Winson's story and worked with her earlier are Vicki Crawford, Marilyn Lowen, James Payne, Sarah Smith, and Alice Walker.

Jewell Dassance, Anita Johnson, Chea Prince, and Kempton Horton contributed their photographs.

Our most profound thanks, of course, is to Jean Fairfax, who recognized over forty years ago the incredible story that lay in the Harmony Community, who spent so much time interviewing Winson and Dovie, and whose transcripts of those interviews served as the primary basis for Winson's voice in the book. Also special gratitude is given to Jane Adams for allowing us to use part of her journal entries to create a vivid picture of life in Harmony during the summer of 1964. The material on the Mississippi Band of Choctaw Indians was drawn from *The Choctaw Revolution*, by Peter J. Ferrara, and we thank Rose Bryan for loaning it to us.

The staffs at the Leake County Library, Leake County Board of Education, Leake County Chamber of Commerce, Chancery Clerk's Office, and Warden Douglas Sproat at the juvenile correctional facility in Walnut Grove provided answers to research questions quickly and kindly.

My personal thanks to: John Dittmer and Charles Bolton for their invaluable scholarly input on Mississippi history; Debbie Gershenowitz at Palgrave for her astute editing ability, understanding of the South, and unfailing humor; Vernon Burton for introducing me to Debbie; Nat

Sobel, my always-supportive agent for ten years now; Emory Women's Studies for continuing to appoint me as a scholar in their program.

Finally, we thank Dovie Hudson and Cleo Hudson, such key actors in this story, whose spirits stood by, both in the telling and the writing.

FOREWORD

Derrick Bell

During the early 1960s, I doubt that I was the only civil rights lawyer who saw him- or herself as the briefcase-carrying counterpart of the Lone Ranger. We flew into Southern cities and towns, prepared our hearings with local counsel, and spoke out fearlessly in courtrooms often filled with hostile whites on one side, and hopeful blacks on the other. Whatever the outcome, we were the heroes to our black clients and their friends and supporters. "Lawyer," they would tell us admiringly, "you sure did stand up to those racists." We were, we thought, breaking down the legal barriers of racial segregation and opening a broad new road toward freedom and justice.

I spent so much time in Mississippi that officials there—as unneeded proof that they were aware of our comings and goings—assessed, and I paid, state income taxes. Those were exciting and sometimes frightening times. But when Northern friends asked me whether I was afraid, I always responded with a question of my own. How could I be afraid to go down and spend several days representing black people who had quite literally put their livelihoods, their homes, and even their lives on the line seeking no more than the rights guaranteed by the Constitution and the simple decency they deserved as citizens, as human beings?

Following that response, those who asked seldom inquired further, but of course I was often afraid for our clients and myself. Even a half-dozen years after the Supreme Court's decision holding as unconstitutional racial segregation in state-run facilities, there were in the deep South legions of whites determined, often violently determined, that the Court's desegregation orders would never be enforced. For them, separate and unequal was more than a racial policy, it was a narcotic under the influence of which even the lowliest white person could feel superior.

Attorney, now Senior federal judge, Constance Baker Motley, and I were in Jackson, Mississippi, on what must have been one of a dozen trips seeking court injunctions barring the University of Mississippi from denying admission to James Meredith. While there, we met with a small delegation of people from rural Leake County. Their spokespersons were Winson and Dovie Hudson, women with purpose in their eyes. They were, we soon learned, the pillars of the Harmony community, and had come seeking our help in getting their school, the Harmony School, reopened. The all-white school board had closed it as a means of intimidating the Harmony community activists who used the school—built by themselves with financial help from the Rosenwald Fund—as a meeting place.

I told them that our crusade was not to save segregated schools, but to eliminate them. And, if they decided to desegregate the schools in Leake County, the NAACP Legal Defense Fund (LDF) would surely represent them. It was an offer they decided to accept, and one both they and I have had reason to regret. Indeed, when back in New York I told the LDF staff about the meeting, they were speechless—and understandably so, given the fierce resistance we faced trying to desegregate the state's premier university. Well, one staffer told me in jest: "Bell, you go on down there and try to desegregate some public schools in Mississippi, and when they shoot your black ass, we will be able to raise all kinds of money at your memorial service." Everyone laughed, but I was serious. Wrong, but serious.

Petitions were signed, plaintiffs selected, and the suit was filed. As Winson Hudson recollects in chapter three, the white opposition, always hostile, turned ugly. Black people were summarily fired from jobs, had mortgages foreclosed, credit withdrawn. Those closely involved with the school suit found they were the special objects of hate by whites and persons to be avoided at all costs by many, but thank goodness not all, blacks. The litigation resulted eventually in an order to desegregate the first grade in the fall of 1964. By that point, tensions were very high. The admission of what would turn out to be but a single child, Deborah Lewis, became the symbol that both blacks and whites recognized would forever alter their future relationships.

Jean Fairfax, through the American Friends Service Committee, provided welcome financial and social support to the Harmony community and their leaders. She did the driving when we traveled together from Jackson to Leake County. She understood that her sense of direction was far better than mine. When I acknowledged as much, she would respond: "Oh Derrick, that's no compliment. Anyone's sense of direction is better than yours." She was right and it was more than a joke. Those trips were not without risks, and making a wrong turn and getting lost could put us in areas where whites did not want us and where we certainly did not wish to be. Jean drove the dusty roads swiftly, surely, and without fear. "No," she said when I asked her whether she was afraid. "That's what God is for."

On one trip to Harmony in the summer before the desegregation order was scheduled to take effect, Mrs. Behonor McDonald, another Harmony leader, told me that despite all the threats, she lived to harass white folks. While disavowing that she was the spokesperson for those in Harmony working for racial reform, it seemed to me that her words accurately reflected their commitment. The goal was organized resistance to racial subjugation, and its harassing effect was likely more potent precisely because they risked so much without either economic or political power and with no certainty that they could change a system that they had known and hated all of their lives.

Those who stood together with the Hudsons avoided discouragement and defeat because at the moment that they determined to resist their oppression, they were triumphant. They understood the value of that triumph to their spirits. It explained the source of courage that fueled their dangerous challenge to the white power structure of that rural Mississippi county. Nothing the all-powerful whites could do would diminish that triumph.

Years later, I was talking to the Hudson sisters at a conference. By that time they had fought and won battles to vote, to integrate public facilities, to get their fair share of government loans and subsidies—mainly through persistence and most of it without litigation. I reminded them of the counsel I had offered when they came to Jackson seeking legal help in reopening their Harmony School. "Looking back," I said, "I wonder whether I gave you the right advice." I may have been seeking sympathy. I didn't get it. "Well Derrick," Winson responded, "I also wondered whether that was the best way to go about it." Then she added, "It's done now. We made it and we are still moving."

Without a commitment from individuals like the Hudsons and their neighbors in Harmony, who were able to overcome fear, discouragement, and defeat after defeat, civil rights lawyers and organizations could have accomplished nothing. And yet, fixated on current problems, there is too little interest in battles past and won; those who labored without concern for credit have, with few exceptions, not been credited.

The Hudson sisters, Dovie and Winson, have been recognized in Leake County and across their home state of Mississippi. Their labors and methods through which they transformed their community using courage and determination deserves a wide audience. It is a remarkable testament to the concept that what should be done can be done.

CHRONOLOGY

1916	Anger Winson Gates is born on November 17 in Harmony, Mississippi, the tenth of thirteen children born to John Gates and Emma Turner.
1924	Winson's mother, Emma, dies in childbirth at age 44.
1936	Winson marries Leroy Cleo Hudson.
1949–1951	Winson teaches school in rural Leake County after receiving teaching certificate.
1954	NAACP legal defense attorneys, with Thurgood Marshall as lead counsel, win *Brown* v. *Board of Education* desegregation case.
1955	White Citizens' Council, dedicated to the "protection and promotion of white supremacy," founded in Indianola, Mississippi.
1959	Leake County School Board announces plan to close Harmony School, consolidating it with other black schools in Thomastown, Carthage, and South Leake.
1961	Medgar Evers organizes Leake County NAACP. Clara Dotson is elected President and Winson is elected vice-president.
1962	U.S. Justice Department sends Frank Schwelb to Carthage to investigate procedures in Leake County voting registrar's office. Winson and her sister Dovie successfully register to vote.
1963	Medgar Evers is assassinated by white supremacist Byron De La Beckwith on June 11.

1964	In April, the Mississippi Freedom Democratic Party (MFDP) is established as an alternative to the all-white Mississippi Democratic Party. In August, Cleo Hudson attends the Democratic National Convention in Atlantic City, New Jersey, as an MFDP delegate.
1964	Harmony Community Center is built with assistance from Freedom Summer volunteers.
1964	In August, the bodies of Freedom Summer volunteers James Chaney, Michael Schwerner, and Andrew Goodman are found in an earthen dam in Neshoba County, which adjoins Leake County. Earlier that summer, Chaney had lived in Winson's home for three weeks, while Schwerner lived in Dovie's home.
1965	Winson appears before the U.S. Commission on Civil Rights in February to speak about harassment of blacks attempting to register to vote.
1965	In August, President Lyndon Johnson signs the Voting Rights Act into law.
1965	Leake County's first Head Start program is established in Harmony. Winson serves in a variety of roles, ranging from personnel officer to cook to custodian.
1966	Voter registration drive in Leake County, with assistance from the Voter Registration Project of Atlanta, nets 1,000 black voters. Student workers are harassed.
1967	Winson, Mississippi State NAACP President Aaron Henry, Charles Evers, and others integrate the Holiday Inn in Clarksdale, Mississippi, while attending an NAACP meeting.
1967	Bombing attempt on Winson's house in November.

1967	Dovie Hudson's house is bombed twice in three months.
1968	Winson and others promote efforts to desegregate all public facilities in Carthage, Mississippi.
1971	Winson's husband Cleo dies.
1971	In the wake of pending legislation on health maintenance organizations, Winson travels to Chicago, where she attends the American Hospital Association's conference on health care delivery and speaks about the lack of adequate medical care for poor, rural Mississippians.
1972	The first annual Harmony Homecoming is held.
1976	Winson travels to Miami, Florida, as a delegate to the Democratic National Convention.
1989	The Mississippi Democratic Party presents Winson with the Fannie Lou Hamer Award.
1989	Winson attends the opening of photographer Brian Lanker's exhibition "I Dream A World: Portraits of Black Women Who Changed America," at the Corcoran Gallery in Washington, D.C. Her photo, taken with Dovie, is featured in the exhibit.
1994	Winson testifies on behalf of Mississippi's poor citizens before President Bill Clinton's Health Reform Task Committee in Washington, D.C.

ILLUSTRATIONS

INTRODUCTION

Constance Curry

Alice Walker wrote in 1969, "Mrs. Winson Hudson, I've come to know well. She is a large handsome woman with bright coppery skin and crisp dark hair. Her eyes are deeply brown and uncommonly alert. When she is speaking to you her eyes hold you; at the same time they seem to be scanning the landscape. Her eyes tell a great deal about Mrs. Hudson, for she is one of the 'sleepless ones' found in embattled Mississippi towns whose fight has been not only against unjust laws and verbal harassment, but against guns and fire bombs as well."[1]

"My sister Dovie's house was bombed twice in November 1967, because of that school mess and because we registered to vote, and our NAACP was always trying to make folks do right. They meant to bomb my house, but we heard the truck. I was night watching until twelve that night, and the Klan was

1. Alice Walker, *In Search of Our Mother's Gardens* (New York: A Harvest/HBJ Book, 1983), p. 14.

backing into our driveway. My daughter, Annie Maude, was living with us while her husband was in Vietnam. She was expecting a baby and was so sick that night, and she heard the truck too. I told her to get up and rush into the back room. My husband Cleo and I got ready to start shooting, but by this time, the German shepherd dog had forced the Klan to move on. I ran to the phone to call Dovie to be ready. When they answered, a bomb went off at her house and I heard Mary, my sister's baby girl, screaming. I started outside and Cleo was shooting, emptying every gun." Winson Hudson tells this story as she recalls her years in a remarkable all-black community—Harmony, Mississippi.

The prevailing national image of the state of Mississippi is the region known as the Delta. The rich, alluvial soil, stretching roughly 150 miles from Memphis to Vicksburg, became home to a plantation society. Here, a white aristocracy emerged, built on the backs of free black labor, and the system made Mississippi the leading cotton-producing state in the country in the nineteenth century. While history and popular culture focus overwhelmingly on the Mississippi Delta, the state is more accurately a study in contrasts. From the sandy beaches of the Gulf Coast to the hill country of the northwest, from the Piney Woods of the southeast to the fertile flatlands of the Delta—home to the blues and the state's largest concentration of black residents—Mississippi varies widely in both geography and culture. A well-entrenched and -documented history of racial oppression singles the state out as an extreme case in the denial of human rights.

After the brief moment of black political participation during Reconstruction, at the turn of the century, the state's African Americans faced a long period of both legal and extralegal disfranchisement. By 1890, Mississippi became the first state to impose a literacy requirement as a precondition to voting. Coupled with outright violence and intimidation, this measure would almost universally overturn the political gains made by blacks after slavery. As in other parts of the South, segregation was enshrined in both law and custom. The state's wide-scale practice of lynching and other forms of violence exceeded that of other Southern states to the extent that Mississippi became the most repressive, totalitarian regime in the South. In addition to the acceptance of violence against blacks, the enactment of discriminatory voting and other laws, the economic system of sharecropping was put into place to allow the continued production of cotton. In many cases sharecropping approached peonage. Blacks, poor whites, and some Native Americans worked a portion of land on large cotton plantations. No salaries were paid, and at the end of the season—settlement time—the "croppers" received an amount of money based on how much cotton they had picked. Their "furnishing" of seeds, tools, and other necessary farming items came from the plantation commissary and their cost was subtracted from their final earnings. Families had little or no control over the final accounting and the majority of the black population remained indebted to white landlords well into the mid-twentieth century. Despite these conditions, a small sector of black independent farmers emerged, along with business owners, and a few professionals scattered in communities throughout the state. From this group came some of the earliest resistance to white supremacy in the dark years of Jim Crow. One small pocket of that resistance was a community in Leake County called Harmony.

Leake County is located in the geographic center of Mississippi, approximately sixty miles from the state capitol in Jackson. It is the only square-shaped county in the state, being exactly twenty-four miles square. It was established in 1833 from territory taken from Choctaw Indians by the federal government, under the Treaty of Dancing Rabbit Creek—a story in itself of injustice and tragedy. Nestled in the heart of this rural county is the all-black community of Harmony—exceptional by Mississippi standards. Harmony, once called Galilee, comprises more than 5,000 acres of land and dates back to the years following the Civil War when former slaves began to purchase land from former slaveholders. Land acquisition continued into the early years of the twentieth century as more African Americans purchased land from local whites who thought it was unfarmable. With their meager earnings from small-scale cotton production, blacks were able to acquire land—sometimes for a dollar an acre—and, over time, some were able to amass substantial portions. As independent landowners, the small farmers of Harmony were never subjected to the economically oppressive conditions of sharecropping. Land ownership provided a sense of personal autonomy, pride, and self-reliance rarely experienced by Delta blacks. When local residents in Harmony did work for whites, it was often to supplement their own earnings from farming.

This was not an area of large plantations, since the land is hilly with some bottoms of good rich soil. Whites usually had small- or medium-sized farms with slaves, but one pervasive thread of "Southern life" did run through Leake County history. White masters raped black slave women, who bore their children, as Winson Hudson tells in her own grandmother's story. The treatment of these children varied, and sometimes they were accepted or acknowledged as relatives of the white families.

And other perversity was always looming. Percy Sanders, descendant of an early black family in the area, recalled hearing as a child about George Slaughter, a white farmer's son by a black woman, who came to a horrible death because "he didn't keep his place." Ambushed by white men, including his own father, he was shot while riding his horse because the saddle horse was "too fine." The story goes that when he was found, "the horse was drinking his blood."

Most of the original black families in Leake County were brought as slaves from Alabama. Percy Sanders' grandfather, Anthony, had been fathered by a Jewish man in Tuscaloosa and brought as a six-month-old infant by his mother. After the Civil War, Percy's father, who had lived with Old Man Jack Sanders, was the first black man to buy land on the Pearl River. By the time Percy was born, on December 25, 1900, his father had accumulated several hundred acres of land. Joe Dotson, Cleo Hudson's grandfather, was another early black landowner who at one time owned about a fourth of the Harmony land. Cleo Hudson and Winson married and later inherited some of that land. It was unusual for blacks not only to accumulate such large tracts of land this early, but also to retain it over the years. Facing a changed economy after the Civil War, some whites were glad to sell land to get the money. They also knew their black neighbors, but as blacks acquired more land, whites moved elsewhere. Some blacks in Harmony, first called Galilee, were reputed to be "tough and mean," and some whites were afraid of the growing sense of community. The story of Harmony is extraordinary because it is a Mississippi story—an account of rural black Mississippians who were taking charge of their lives decades before the civil rights movement of the 1960s.

Similar to other African Americans during Reconstruction and thereafter, residents of this black enclave were in strong pursuit of education. This drive for education had persisted from slavery times, when it was against the law to teach a slave to read and write. The white power structure and blacks from the very beginning knew that educating a black person might give him a way out of the fields. As often quoted in the black community, "Keep us ignorant and we stay in our place." In the 1890s, Northern white philanthropic groups, including the Peabody Educational Fund, the Anna T. Jeanes Fund, and the Julius Rosenwald Fund, provided financial resources for building, monitoring, and other assistance for schools for black children. The Rosenwald contribution to these schools was generally about 15 to 20 percent of the total costs, with the remainder coming from public funds, white contributions, and the contributions of the black school patrons themselves—often described as a system of "double taxation" for blacks. Between 1913 and 1932, the Julius Rosenwald Fund helped establish more than 5,000 schools in the South. In Mississippi, 557 schools for black children received help from the Fund, and in the mid-1920s, about one-fourth of all black children attending school in the state went to a so-called Rosenwald School.

In the Harmony area, organizing activities for a school were centered in the Missionary Baptist Galilee Church, and residents sought out the Rosenwald Fund to help construct the Harmony School. Parents and community members purchased the land for the school from a local black landowner, Sam Kirkland. It was built by the labor and love of the Harmony people, who hauled wood from nearby towns and hamlets and donated their time to construct the building on a hill near Galilee Road. Winson Hudson's aunt, Callie Kirkland Dotson, was able to give cash money to help build the school. She was drawing a check from the government for her son who was killed in World War I. One story says that when the school was finished, she told the people, "Now let us live and work in harmony," and thereafter the Galilee area was known as "Harmony." Completed around 1922, the Harmony School was run by a board of trustees elected from the community. The county paid the teachers, but the trustees hired them. In 1928, a department of vocational education opened, and the first high school graduating class finished that year at the Harmony Vocational High School. Cleo Hudson, Winson's husband, was in that class.

From the outset, the Harmony School was the pride of the community, known for its success in educating its children, until the desegregation challenge in the 1950s threatened its existence. In 1954, the U.S. Supreme Court ruled in *Brown* v. *the Board of Education* that separate schools for blacks and whites are "inherently unequal," and Brown II, in 1955, mandated implementation of the ruling, "with all deliberate speed." Mississippi and other segregated school systems scrambled to upgrade and improve all-black schools to show that blacks were indeed getting equal education. By 1959, the Leake County School Board planned to consolidate the Harmony School with black schools in nearby communities. The Board's vote to close the Harmony School precipitated organizing efforts in Harmony, the establishment of an NAACP chapter, and the first school desegregation suit filed in a rural Mississippi county. Winson worked to help her sister, Dovie, in 1961, to file that first lawsuit. Dovie's daughter, Diane, was the plaintiff.

Harmony has remained a tight-knit black community where families pass along land from one generation to the next. The tenacious spirit of Harmonites fostered a culture of resistance to white domination and control that, by the late 1950s, coalesced into a remarkable, indigenous leadership in the state's black freedom struggle. As the struggle spread from schools to voting to economic rights, Harmony residents with determined leadership, including Winson, her husband Cleo, and sister Dovie, helped pave the way for change in Leake County. In 1964, during Freedom Summer, young volunteer civil rights workers came to Harmony to live and support the local programs. As in other communities across the state, Freedom Summer brought black voter registration and political organization, increased economic opportunities, emphasis on black education, and other lasting changes, and it left a legacy of renewed hope in Harmony.

Mississippi Harmony is a first-person account by Winson Hudson, native of Harmony. She tells of fights on many fronts in the black freedom struggle in the last half of the twentieth century. Born on November 17, 1916, she has lived her 86 years in Harmony, through some of the most racially oppressive periods in the state's history, including the legalized segregation of the Jim Crow era, the recurrence of harassment and organized resistance to school desegregation in the 1950s, the tumultuous days of the 1960s freedom struggle, and the day-to-day more subtle, sometimes hidden battles of the last forty years. During most of her adult life, Winson also faced rejection and opposition by some people in the black community, themselves oppressed economically and terrorized over the years by white intimidation and Klan violence.

While fighting for school desegregation in 1961, Winson helped found the Leake County NAACP, in which she served for thirty-eight years (1962–2001) as its president. Challenges in 1961 from Winson and other residents of Harmony on the state's practice of black disfranchisement resulted in one of the first U.S. Justice Department investigations into voting procedures in Leake County. After having attempted to register numerous times, beginning in 1937, she finally met the state's literacy requirement. In 1962, in response to a question on the meaning of a passage in the state constitution, she answered, "It said what it meant and it meant what it said." This was finally good enough to pass the test.

The narrative of Winson Hudson and the Harmony community is both triumphant and tragic, inspiring and disturbing. It is the history of an extraordinary yet recognizable woman whose strength and courage helped define an entire new era in American history. As with many African American women who led the black freedom struggle in local communities across the South, the role and activism of Winson and her sister Dovie have not been fully known or understood. The overemphasis on national civil rights leadership has brought limited knowledge of the women who, along with young people, comprised a large number of movement participants. Women's activism was more pronounced on the local and regional levels, where they were often the first to attempt voter registration or house "outside" civil rights workers.

As in the case of Winson and Dovie Hudson, for many female activists, civil rights was an extension of broader community work, whether it was for health care, government loans, telephone service, good roads, housing, or child care. As they understood it, all of these issues were intertwined with the black freedom struggle and the challenge to racial exclusion. Winson Hudson's local community work and successes drew attention from state and national groups, and she became a recognized and trusted spokesperson at political and advocacy meetings all over the country.

I first met Winson Hudson in 1964 when I was working for the American Friends Service Committee, a Quaker service organization, based in Philadelphia, with a long history of worldwide human rights work. My AFSC colleague, Jean Fairfax, was the director of the Southern Civil Rights Program for the national office and spent time working with the black communities in Jackson, Biloxi, and Leake County, all under court order to desegregate schools in the fall of 1964. Jean was working specifically with attorney Derrick Bell, of the New York NAACP Legal Defense and Educational Fund, on these cases. They visited Leake County often, and Jean took me up to meet Winson and her sister Dovie.

Later, in 1989, I accompanied Jean when she visited Harmony and began recording interviews with Winson. Jean was aware of Winson's long and dedicated battles on so many fronts, and we both have stayed in touch with her over the years. I, too, have been continually amazed by her integrity and the consistency of her struggle. She was a friend of Mae Bertha Carter, another civil rights leader up in the Delta, whose story I told in my book *Silver Rights.* They sometimes traveled and spoke together before Mae Bertha's death in 1999.

Winson first began recording her story on paper and audiocassettes in the late sixties and has been interviewed by many scholars, friends, and family since then. The account of her life and activism has been preserved and recorded here in her own voice, supported when needed by a broader history of events and circumstances in the Mississippi struggle. The book is arranged thematically (although it generally follows chronological lines) because Winson's experiences provide a valuable window into understanding key aspects of the struggle for black equality. Historical background appears in italics, at the beginning of each chapter. When necessary, additional information to assist the reader with context in included in brackets.

When Winson first asked me to build on the work of others and help finish her book while she could "see it and touch it," I could not say no. She has been waiting so long for her story to be told. It has been an honor and a pleasure to work with Winson and with her extended family in Harmony and the rest of the country. Some of the rural roads in and around Harmony still remain unpaved, and in many ways, to visit Harmony is to travel back in time. There are a growing number of small strip malls; the enormous, brightly lit Choctaw Maid Farms poultry plant that resembles a casino at first glance; and a Wal Mart in the nearby town of Carthage. Two thriving casinos, hotels, businesses, and schools are in neighboring Neshoba County, owned and managed by the Choctaw Band of Indians, and a new, private Youth Correctional Facility in Walnut Grove represents another kind of growth. But the Harmony community remains relatively obscure, nestled in the sand hills of Leake County. The surrounding area is still home to white farmers, and blacks and whites, Choctaws and an increasing Hispanic population maintain a sometimes uneasy peace among themselves.

Many from Harmony's earlier generation are no longer living and have passed down land to new generations. Some of them are coming home after living in the North and West, and new frame and brick houses are built or under construction on

Harmony roads. For these newcomers, the early days of segregation and extreme discrimination are but remnants of days gone by—stories rarely passed on by older relatives. Winson has told her story to remind them and us of her own struggles and the continuing struggle of her people.

Several key themes emerge in Winson's life and appear again and again: family, community, and land—themes that have persisted in the hearts and struggles of African Americans since slavery. Without fanfare, financial wealth, or educational titles, Winson fought these three battles along with many others. One of the white volunteers in 1964 described her summer in Harmony: "We live with fear as a condition like heat or night." Winson Hudson had to accept this fear for a lifetime. Her wisdom, humor, and deep political commitment define a life that helped change the course of events in the twentieth century.

Chapter One

"THE BEST OF TIMES . . . THE WORST OF TIMES": YOUTH

Anger Winson Gates Hudson was born in Harmony, Mississippi, on November 17, 1916, the tenth of the thirteen children born to John Wesley Gates and Emma Kirkland. Winson was named after her paternal grandmother, Angeline Gates Turner. Winson called her "Grandma Ange." She was Winson's link to the past and kept alive the memories of slavery and life before and after the Civil War. When Angeline Gates Turner was four years old, in 1840, she was brought to Leake County, Mississippi, from Tuscaloosa, Alabama. She grew up a slave in the home of the Moore family. When one of the Moore daughters married a Gates, young Angeline was given to the daughter. Angeline took the name of Gates and worked as a house servant until she married George Turner. She was almost 100 years old when she died.

The courage and strength of Grandma Ange made an indelible imprint on Winson and helped to form the woman she would become. Winson's father was also key in teaching her to stand up for her rights. Winson was eight when her mother died, and her father singlehandedly raised eleven of the thirteen children. Their farm of 105 acres provided food and resources for the family until a white doctor who had loaned them money took the land in payment and sold it to another black family. Winson's activism as a grassroots civil rights and community organizer evolves from her early childhood and young adult years growing up in rural Mississippi as the daughter and granddaughter of proud black people who dared to create a world of their own. Winson Hudson has vivid recollections of the stories passed along from her grandmother and of growing up in Harmony.

The Moore family bought Grandma Ange when she was five. She was always right around the big house and waited on Mrs. Moore—they called her "Ole Miss." She told us that they trained her to be a "house nigger," and that she did have it a little better than the people in the field, who got whippings. She got all the family secrets and would always tell the slaves out in the field what was going on—how to get away—when to get away. Then she'd run back and tell the master—"You'd better go, so-and-so's trying to get away." But they had already gone, and she'd pretend she didn't know a thing—and a lot of them got away from the master by what Grandma Ange had told them. She had good ears and listened a lot. If she heard that they were going to whip Ed Sanders, the slave that was in charge of the other slaves, she would slip away and tell Ed.

Here are some of my favorite stories from Grandma Ange. One night she heard the mistress and master crying and ran to see what she could do. They told her the North and South were in a war and the master would have to go. If the North won, they would make them let Ange go, and told her, "you will have to get out on your own, get food and clothes the best way you can." Grandma told us, "I started crying too, but my heart was leaping with joy as I listened to master talk about the war. Then, for the first time, they started giving me plenty of food, and mistress seemed afraid and treated me better and better. It was a great time. I stayed in the house with mistress, and I didn't know where I would go if I was free, but I thought of those other slaves who worked like oxen, men and women, and some had gotten old, and late in the evening I could hear them hollering and crying. One morning Ole Miss called me to her room and said that the North had whipped the South and the master had been killed in battle, and now she'd have to let me go free. Later master came home."

Grandma would lay on a pallet in their room to take care of the baby if it cried at night, so Ole Miss wouldn't have to get up. She would rock the baby for stomach trouble—lots of babies had it back then and some died—it was called colitis. She was known, even until she died, as a fortune-teller. But, what she would do is eavesdrop on the master and Ole Miss talking, and they would think she was just a little child, not paying attention to anything. Then later she would start breaking down in tears and telling them what she had seen in a dream. She'd moan and say, "Oh, Missy, Missy—I had a dream that this terrible thing was going to happen," and it would be things that she had heard 'em say, and she would stir up a big rigmarole about it. Ole Miss kind of believed Angeline and was a little afraid of her. They felt like she was a foreseer.

In addition to a foreseer, Grandma Ange was known to go out and get herbs and doctor babies during this time. She had a healing hand. Once an old man had a sore that wouldn't heal. She went out and got some rosin off of pine trees and mixed it up with boiling tea and plastered it on that sore and it healed up. She would take that big leaf that looks like an elephant ear and put it on your head for a fever and it would ease it. She'd make tea for sick babies too, and as long as she lived, even my mother's generation and my generation, did exactly what Grandma Ange said as far as making teas and such. Grandma Ange went all over this community and out of the community delivering babies—white and black. They'd come and get her on a horse or in their buggy—rain, snow, or sleet. She was very popular as a midwife and once she saved a baby everyone had given up on—very few babies she lost.

Grandma Ange married George Turner, and we all called him "Pappy." He and Grandma Ange looked like pure Africans. Pappy was bought in Alabama and brought to Leake County. He didn't talk about things like Grandma, but he did tell us that his whole family was sold off—all to different places. He never heard from any of them and he died wanting to go back to Alabama. He had had many beatings, but he wanted to go back to see if his Ma was there or if he could find some of his family.

My own father loved Pappy and Grandma Ange so much. He moved them near us so that he could help care for them. He would have us, the little children, carry a bucket of cool water to the field to Pappy. Whenever the bucket was empty, he would beat it like a drum and sing his song, "I'm going away to Alabama, dili, dili, dom, dom, going away to Alabam, dili, dili, dom, dom, dom." Sometimes he would stop singing and pat his hands and laugh, and we knew he was happy. But if he looked up and saw someone coming he would shut up—working hard from daylight to dark and sometimes seeming like a fearful man.

Grandma just told so much, and she sung songs too, like the one about old Massa went away and the darkies stayed at home. She'd sing, "You're old enough and big enough—you ought to know better than to meet him on the way." What she was saying was that master went away, and while he was gone, you better be careful to dodge him—so hit the woods if you run away. I remember songs like this and stories, too, where we would sit for hours on the porch. We had a big old house—there were about six or seven rooms. And we didn't have no newspaper, no radios, or nothing. And everybody would eat and get out on the porch and listen to Grandma Ange tell her stories. And they stuck with me.

She told us more about Ed Sanders, the slave who ran the farm. Ole Master finally killed him. He wasn't able to work any more and Ole Master just hit him in the head. After he killed him, Ed came back and he didn't have no head and he hainted [haunted] Ole Master until he died himself—getting in his way all the time—Ole Ed would be right there with him. And not only Ed came back. Different slaves that Ole Master threatened or killed came back in the form of a white dog. Dog would get in front of Ole Master and not let him by and everywhere he went, white dog would be sitting with him. Grandma Ange said, "Ole Master just couldn't rest nowhere."

When my father would hear Grandma Ange sitting in the twilight telling us stories on the porch, he would tell her to stop. He didn't want us to be afraid and told us there was nothing to them and no such things as ghosts. Grandma Ange then said, "Shut up John, I'm just telling these children, they'd better be good to folk, or they'll come back to haint you." But my father always told us, "Don't worry about nothing, because I'll take care of you. Just do the right thing." And see, that grew up in us, and there's not a one of

1. Winson's grandmother (r), Angeline Turner (Grandma Ange), and her niece, Mandy Bright, 1929. Personal collection of Winson Hudson.

us in the family that's afraid of anything. My sisters and my brother—it's a wonder we hadn't gotten killed. We would just stand up and say whatever we wanted to.

When Grandma went to town in Carthage she was real tough. She went in a store once and bought her a bunch of groceries and she didn't have no money. So she just walked out. And the store merchant was white. He said, "Angeline, you didn't pay me for this stuff you got." Grandma said, "Pshaw! I ain't going to give you nothing, boy. I brought you into this world, and I ain't never got a penny for it. I ain't never got nothing. I didn't charge your folks nothing 'cause they didn't have nothing. I ain't going to pay you nothing for this." And he just left her alone, 'cause she delivered him. That was a white man.

Grandma Ange also told me a lot about being a black girl growing up. She and my grandfather, Pappy George Turner, were really devoted to each other. I heard her once say how proud she was to be able to marry a dark-skinned man—that she was "sick and tired of white folks." See, three of her children were born before her marriage to Pappy George Turner and two of them were by white men. Grandma Ange had nine children in all, eight boys and one girl. They were Whitfield, John Wesley, Topp, Lela, Ernest, Rodney, Charles, Ace, and Alonzo. The oldest son, Whitfield Gates, and my father, John Wesley Gates, were by two white men. My father and Uncle Whitfield looked like Indians. The third son was by a black man we called Uncle Topp. The two white men were brothers from the Moore family, who had brought Grandma Ange as a slave to Leake County, and they both took advantage of her and each one of them had a child by her. My father's father was Dave Moore, a lawyer, and Whitfield's was a merchant—ran a big store in town. Grandma was always proud of her large family—back then, you didn't count for much if you didn't have lots of children. Some families had twelve and thirteen children—lots of hands to work.

Now, those two white Moore brothers didn't have much to do with their black children, but their sister, Luna Moore, did. That would have been my daddy's auntie—a white woman who took a liking to Grandma Ange. When Grandma Ange went over to Carthage, she would visit Luna Moore and Luna would give her clothes and food to bring back and give her something to eat. Grandma Ange wanted me to be like Luna Moore. She was real smart for that time; she owned a typewriter. Grandma would say to me, "Get your books and read your books, and be like Luna Moore. One of these days, you'll be able to write with your fingers and that means that you'll be able to write with a typewriter. And then, you'll be able to ride on an airship and fly over the trees and everything just like a bird." Now, wasn't no such thing as an airplane back then, but Grandma had heard about one and had been exposed to things through Luna Moore and her dealings with white folks over in Carthage.

Sometimes, white wives would kind of try halfway and have a little something to do with these children their white men had with black women, but the white men would have nothing to do with them. My father went by the last name of Gates, but my father always said that he loved Pappy George Turner like his own father, and Pappy never did make any difference between him and his own children, who were all very dark-skinned.

You know some of them white Moore offspring are still around here, but they sure don't own us any more. They're just like the Barnett and the Hudson folks, and I'm talking about Governor Ross Barnett's people. He was the governor that wouldn't let James Meredith come to Ole Miss in 1962, because he was black. They had a big riot there, and people were killed on that campus. Ross himself is a relative on my husband's side. We never had much pressure either way from Governor Ross Barnett or his family. One of those Barnett cousins—they were nice to us at first—even invited us over to the Barnett Manor up the road at Standing Pine.

Dovie's husband was Arden Hudson, and he and my husband and my sister Alice's husband are all cousins—three sisters married the first cousins. So that's why me and Dovie are both Hudsons. And our husbands were both related to the Barnetts, and all of 'em looked like Barnetts. If you'd see the pictures, you'd know they was kin. Their grandmother, Sally Hudson—you couldn't know no way that she was a black woman. She married a black man, and some of their children were dark. But my husband's father and Dovie's husband's father was real light, and we figure that's where the Barnetts came in. That's why this "race" and color business don't make no sense.

Grandma Ange told me that I would never have to go through days like those she had gone through before she married Pappy. And she would say over and over, "Don't let these white men run over you." At the time, I was too young to know what she meant, but as I got to be a young lady, I knew exactly what she meant. Back then, white boys would rape you and then come and destroy the family if you said anything about it. You would just have to accept it. They were liable to come in and run the whole family off. I couldn't walk the roads at anytime alone for fear I might meet a white man or boy. I couldn't walk the street without some white man winking his eye or making some sort of sound. This made me so angry because I had five brothers, and I heard my father almost daily warning them against even

2. Barnett family mansion in Standing Pine, Leake County. Governor Ross Barnett and Cleo Hudson shared some of the same relatives. Personal collection of Constance Curry.

walking near a white girl or looking at them or going near a house unless they knew that white men were there too.

So, I had as little contact with white men as possible. Now, some black women worked as maids for white families around here, but not any from the Harmony community. A few Harmony folks would go out and pick cotton for whites from time to time in order to buy school clothes and such, but my daddy wouldn't let a one of his girls do that—not a single day. When we did work away from home, you'd better believe that it was a bunch of us or some boys with us—not by ourselves—at no time. They really protected the women. Because, you know, if a girl went through a trail or to the spring—there wasn't no roads like now—just a little wagon road, and if you were by yourself and met a white man, you just were almost sure to be raped.

Also, at this time, many black men were being lynched. Pappy and Grandma had already lost a son, Alonzo. She grieved for him, her fourth son, who was born mentally retarded and hanged for supposedly killing a white man. He was working for the man, and the whites claimed that Alonzo knocked this white man in the head. The white man was killed, but Alonzo always said that he didn't do it. He said that the mules ran away and knocked the man down—that's what he always told my father and his brother. But the whites eventually took him. Alonzo tried to run away, and they caught him, not too far from where I live right now. After they caught him, nobody knew about the trial or anything, but they set him on his coffin and carried him off to the hanging ground by the river. Yep, made him ride on his own coffin. The hanging rope went up and over the bridge and after the hanging they cut the rope into pieces and sold them for souvenirs. That was around 1916 or so; I was still a baby. My father and grandma were so mad about this, but they didn't talk about it much. They were afraid and wouldn't have nothing much to say.

One man they hung not too far from here and burnt him too. Said he was riding a too fine saddle horse. His daddy was a white man, and his daddy was in the mob. This was common around here; it never will be told just how many young boys disappeared too. Just kill 'em and throw 'em in the pond and laugh about it. People were so afraid, because the whites considered lynching legal—hanging in trees, burning alive. That's one reason we got support for the NAACP—they were trying to eliminate lynching, and it made some folks be able to send for their boys to come home—boys sent up North to stay alive.

My father was a good man and one of the bravest men I believe I have ever seen. He believed in human rights and dignity, although his rights were always denied to him. He respected the rights of all people—even the rights of a child. My mother, Emma Laura Kirkland Gates, died at the age of forty-four here in Leake County when I was still only eight years old. She died from a lack of medical attention while giving birth. This was common back then. People had nothing like birth controls. It was just no other choice but to have children. Her death could have been prevented if the doctor had put her on a diet instead of letting her eat fattening food. She had been in labor so long at the time she passed. She was at home and had complications and it was just no way to get that baby from her but to let her die. There wasn't no hospitals for blacks in those very early days and no funeral homes. The baby lived to be fourteen. My grandmother Ange was the midwife, but the baby was so large that she couldn't handle my mother's delivery. They had to call in a white doctor and he wasn't nice. I remember when my mother was giving birth, the doctor insisted on keeping her propped up. He said to take the pillow out from under her and elevate her body with her head down. She said that she felt like she was smothering to death. I don't know whether her lying down would have saved her, but the doctor would not let her lie down.

My father had 105 acres in Harmony and that same white doctor held a bank note against our land. Like so many black people we had to borrow money from white people for seeds and supplies and farm equipment, and they would hold a bank note against the land. We probably could have waited to pay if my father had done what the doctor said and let some of us daughters work for him, but my father said no, and we finally lost our land to him. But later he sold it to a black man 'cause white folks wouldn't want to live in Harmony.

There were thirteen of us children at the time my mother died, and my father took care of them all. There was Quellie, Willie, Glover, Alice, Fletcher, Frazier, Raymond, Ollie, Dovie, Winson, Osly, Marvin, and Melvin. Two of my sisters, Willie and Ollie, died in childbirth too. Willie was only seventeen years old. In those days, a lot of families ran their girls off from home if they got pregnant, and sometimes the daddies who ran them off had women on the side themselves and they had outside children of their own. But, my parents didn't believe in that. Still, Willie didn't want to bring no disgrace on the family, so she went down to Arkansas with my mother's sister, Aunt Myrt, and she died there trying to have the baby. My mother never got over it; she grieved her daughter's death.

3. Winson's father, Reverend John Wesley Gates, ca. 1928. Personal collection of Winson Hudson.

Later, Ollie died giving birth to her sixth child. She laid in the hospital and the baby was dead for days, and she just laid there with the dead baby inside of her. That was the worst thing I ever heard of. And when she was almost dead, they went and took that baby. That was Melvin. She didn't even realize it. She laid there so long until she was out of her mind. She sung and she prayed, and she talked to her other children and told 'em what to do just like my mother did—how to live, and what to do and to hold yourself together and go on to school, because they were all small children at the time.

Ollie was in the colored section of a hospital in Newton County, Mississippi. That was a terrible death, there. Dovie and me were with her when she was dying. We slept on the floor and they wouldn't even give us a pillow. I can still hear Ollie singing, "Whiter than snow, the beautiful snow, He has made me," and then she would take a breath, and sing, "O Lord, O Lord, I'm in your care. Put your loving arms around me, so my enemies cannot harm me. O Lord, O Lord, I'm in your care." And then she took another breath, and then she'd sing some more and then she died. Some of my other siblings died from lack of medical care, and others have passed over the years and that leaves only two of us, me and Osly, still alive.

Growing up in the Harmony community was both the best of times and the worst in some ways. Before we lost our land to that white doctor, we raised everything to feed our family—corn and other vegetables, and then cane to make syrup. We had to work so hard trying to make a living farming, and some families had to go elsewhere to find work.

Dovie and her eleven children went to Crownville, Louisiana, to help a white farmer with cotton, corn, and soybean crops. Sometimes they stayed there a long time and sometimes they would come back and forth to Harmony. In our family, my daddy had something for us to do every day, all the time. And on the weekends, we would meet up somewhere and go visit each other. Families would spend the entire day at each other's houses. And, on Sunday, we'd look forward to these big families visiting each other—all my momma's sisters, bringing the children and making pallets for them and all spending the night. We would cook up big old dinner pots of peas and a great big old pie. And those children would eat. Didn't have meats and a balanced menu, but them big families would eat. Syrup cakes and teacakes and vegetables and big old pans of cornbread and everybody got full. Then, the next Sunday, it'd be time to go to the other one's house. We'd look forward to that—the whole family—men and women and children. Didn't have nowhere else to go.

The church was the center of my life in many respects. All my folks was religious—my mother was a missionary before she died, and my father was a minister, so I stayed in church all my life. We went to Sunday school every Sunday and church once a month. Then we came home from Sunday school and had dinner. I became part of a little group—the young people's Red Circle—when I got big enough. We had the family visits, but my parents didn't let us date much when we were teenagers. I had my first boyfriend when I was sixteen years old, but until then, I was a tomboy. My daddy really just let me climb trees and ride horses, because I was kind of tomboyish, and everybody said I was "bad." I could ride a bucking horse, and I could kill a hog or anything just like a man. I played with boys and girls, but I never did fight.

I wasn't the type to fight. I wasn't afraid, but my father taught us not to fight. I broke up fights by talking. And my brothers and sisters never really fought either. We loved each other so much. When we sat down to eat, it was eleven of us, and nobody would eat until everybody got to the table. Everyone would say a Bible verse before we ate. My father didn't believe in whipping either. A lot of people at that time thought that was what it took to raise children. But my father sat down and would talk to you and you'd almost rather him whip you than to look you in the face and talk to you. He would say, "Why did you hurt me like that?" He'd say over and over how something hurt him and how much he loved me. The preacher might get up and say, "Spare the rod and spoil the child" and people would clap and holler "amen." But my father never went along with that.

When I got to be around sixteen, I did start keeping company with boys, but it wasn't like they're doing now. Your company had to leave at 8:00 P.M., and then you had to sit where somebody could see you and leave the door open. There wasn't no way to ride, unless you'd go out in a wagon. If your boyfriend walked you to the house, you'd better believe there were four or five relatives and friends there, some in front and some in the back. You didn't have a chance. Now, some people had better breaks than others, but my daddy was strict and he didn't allow us to dance or sing the blues. Sometimes, he let the boys go off in the field where they would holler and sing the blues. Us girls just sang religious songs. Every now and then, though, I would slip off and dance and sing the blues.

Growing up in Harmony, since we were all related mostly, it was hard to find somebody to court and marry. I had two families to choose from—maybe three, and that included only some of the Langdons because other Langdons were first cousins. Now, the Hudson folks in Leake County and the Striblings were not related, but they didn't have no boys. You couldn't marry your first cousin. That wasn't a law, just a community feeling. Some married their third cousins and such as that, but it was too close if you married your first cousin. But, you couldn't hardly find nobody to marry in here, and the only time you got exposed to other men was once a year in September. The Lone Pilgrim Convention was an association of about eighteen churches, and each year they would have a convention where people from all over Leake County would meet and some from neighboring counties. You would get to meet a whole lot of young men—just about as many men as women. But you had to be careful—our men, back then, said others better be careful—they weren't gonna let nobody come in here and take their girls. It's not like today—when there aren't many young black men and a whole lot of them in jail, killing themselves on drugs sold by white men.

I met my future husband, Cleo Hudson, at the convention. His grandfather, Joe Dotson, owned four or five hundred acres in Harmony. We married during the Depression years in 1936, when cotton was as low as five cents per pound. Day work was seventy-five cents per day. My husband and I had it hard trying to survive here during those times. Finally, around 1940, we locked up our doors and went to Chicago to his brother Rufus's home. Cleo got a job for $15.00 a week, and I got a job with my sister-in-law for $10.00 a week at Oak Park Hospital in Oak Park, Illinois. This hospital was just as segregated as the ones in Mississippi and there was always somebody standing around to give you orders. I didn't like that—blacks left out in Chicago as well as in Mississippi. Cleo was unhappy too, so we decided to make our way back home to Mississippi. Both of us

4. Winson and Cleo Hudson, Chicago, 1946. Personal collection of Winson Hudson.

liked fishing and hunting and much of our living came from game. We had to work so hard just to hold on. We were home for a while, but hard times forced us to go back to Chicago and try again. We stayed one year. By this time we were caring for Annie Maude, Cleo's niece, and we didn't like leaving our baby daughter with a babysitter while we worked, so we packed up and came home to die.

Something good happened to me this time when I came home from Chicago the second time, around 1950. A neighbor, Mattie Ree Sanders, came to our house one night and asked me if I wanted to teach school with her. I told her that I needed a job, but I didn't think I was qualified to teach school. I had left school in the eleventh grade, when me and Cleo got married. Mattie said that all I needed was a little work experience and then I could get a license. I did this and we worked at a little school called Bay Spring Grammar School, about eight miles from Harmony. I had the first, second, third, and fourth grades and Mrs. Sanders taught the fifth, sixth, seventh, and eighth. Both of us put out all we had trying to help the children to learn. Most of the boys just came to school on rainy days, and most all the children stayed out until all the cotton was picked.

By this same time, the Harmony School had been long-established and it was one of the best schools in this area. I wanted to see the children at nearby Bay Spring come to the Harmony School. The Board of Education came up with a consolidation plan. Mr. C. R. Murphy had been hired as principal of the Harmony School, and Mrs. Sanders and I worked with him to bring Bay Spring School and another little school, Mt. Calvary, into the Harmony School, and it became so strong. Mrs. Sanders and Mrs. Ward were hired as teachers, and I took a job as Assistant Lunchroom Manager. Students from adjoining counties came in and boarded in private homes here in Harmony. With three black trustees to run the school, elections were held the first Saturday in March of each year. The Parent Teacher Association (PTA) played a vital part in running the school and I served as President for several years. So, teachers had to do their jobs or get fired. The Harmony School was our pride and the center of the community.

As a lunchroom worker, we served food that mostly came from government commodities: dry beans, powdered eggs, dry milk, peanut butter, cheese. Lunches were fifteen cents, but fifteen cents was hard to get in those days. Some of the children would be so hungry at lunchtime they would just stand around the lunchroom. So we used a large wood stove and several bread pans and I would make up enough bread to give those children a large piece of bread and butter. One teacher caught me handing out bread to the children and reported me to the principal. The principal called me in and I told him how hungry these children were and the bread and butter were not costing us anything since they came from government commodities. He said, "You can't feed these children free." I felt so bad to have to go back and tell those hungry children that we couldn't give out bread any more. But, I still would put bread in a bag and tell them to get away from the lunchroom to eat it.

Working in the schools made me understand about the battles we'd have to fight in education and food and health care and helped prepare me for the good chances coming in the freedom movement of the 1960s.

Chapter Two

"IT SAID WHAT IT MEANT AND IT MEANT WHAT IT SAID": VOTER REGISTRATION

When Winson and other black citizens attempted to register in Leake County in the 1960s, they faced a wall of diehard opposition, dating back to Reconstruction. "Leake County History: Its People and Places" (compiled by Mackie and Louise Spence, Curtis Media Corporation, 1984) records the legacy, as told by early residents, dating back to the times following the civil war. "Election day was a great event for the negroes. They would march to the polls in great droves, having been supplied with ballots several days in advance. The carpetbaggers, scalawags, and negroes outnumbered the Democrats, yet in the three campaigns in which they put out tickets, in 1866, 1871, and 1872, they never carried an election. The principle for which the Democrats stood was white supremacy. . . . The Republican ticket contained a very conspicuous U.S. flag on the back. . . . This enabled negroes to detect [it] anywhere. The negroes held secret meetings just before elections and were well posted by their respective leaders. The different companies or negro clubs would dress in uniform, and at the sound of the drum march in a body to the polls, but they did not always succeed.

"At an election in Thomastown, in 1866, when a troop of these would-be voters presented themselves, George Nash placed himself on the gallery of an old store, in full view of the polling place, with a pistol in his hand, and said he would shoot the first black man who tried to vote. The blacks knew him well enough to take him at his word and immediately began to scatter. The shed room of this old store had been filled with guns to use in case of emergency."

The account continues to describe the 1871 election, when the constable of that beat kept count of the number of "Negroes" who voted and then carried the ballot box to a private home, opened it, dumped the contents into the fire, refilled it with Democratic votes, and returned to the voting place where the election continued. Cheating blacks out of their vote became a sign of patriotism among whites. On one occasion, the tally sheets showed how many votes were in the ballot box, and "stuffers" took the box, and in a quick switch, put in Democratic tickets and left a few Republican tickets for appearance's sake. As the History says, "This was the most satisfactory plan ever worked out in Leake County."

Ned Rushing, a black Baptist minister in Leake County who tried to help his black brothers at the ballot box, was whipped by white men and given a "red shirt, by the use of long hickories actively applied." In the election of 1872, the Democrats regained control, and "the carpetbag rule was forever destroyed in Leake County."

The tactics of intimidation and violence to prevent black voting and political participation were used throughout Mississippi, and by 1890, the state constitutional convention was admittedly geared to disfranchise blacks and to counteract gains made by blacks under Reconstruction. The most damaging of the "legal" barriers were the literacy requirements. In order to register, applicants were required to copy any section of the Mississippi Constitution chosen by the registrar, and then write an interpretation of the section. White U.S. Senator from Mississippi, Theodore Bilbo, said in 1946: "The poll tax won't keep 'em from voting. What keeps 'em from voting is section 244 of the Constitution of 1890. . . . It says that a man to register must be able to read and explain the Constitution or explain the Constitution when read to him. . . . A Constitution that damn few white men and no niggers at all can explain." The tests were administered by white registrars and people passed or failed at their sole discretion. Those rejected had no recourse.

Almost a century after Reconstruction, pervading white fears of black political participation and control continued. Tactics for continuing disfranchisement of blacks were just a little less overt. In 1954, only 5 percent of the black population in Leake County was registered to vote. In 1962, the Justice Department sent representatives to Leake County to investigate complaints from black people on the denial of their right to vote. Two of them, Bob Owen and Frank Schwelb, found that rejected black applicants had been asked to interpret Section 241 of the state Constitution—a provision of 206 words that defined, in legal terms, the technical qualifications for voting in Mississippi. White people were asked to interpret Section 240—nine words—"All elections shall be by ballot." They also found that of the 200 registered blacks (out of more than 5,000 eligible) not one had been registered from 1955 through the end of 1961. At one point during their investigation, a deputy sheriff approached Owen and Schwelb and after verifying they were the "ones from Washington," said, "You know, you can give a nigger a million dollars, you can put him through Harvard, but he's still nothin' more than a plain ole nigger."

Frank Schwelb's notes from that time indicate that after the agreement with county officials, maybe a few hundred Negro applicants were registered. Among those first newly registered were Mr. and Mrs. Junior Smith of Ofahoma, whose son Ferr, a young college student, had written to Attorney General Robert Kennedy in 1962, pleading with him to do something about the unfair treatment for blacks who were trying to register in Leake County.

Interventions and investigations by the Justice Department accompanied by the continuing voter registration efforts by the freedom movement across the South led to the passage of the Voting Rights Act of 1965, which prohibited circuit clerks from using the practices that had kept blacks from registering to vote.

In the meantime, it took Winson and Dovie Hudson many tries, over many years, to register to vote.

When I was growing up way back then in the 1920s, we didn't have no newspapers and no radios and no television in Harmony, so black people didn't know about voting anyway—just do what the big white folks told us to do. I don't ever remember my father being able to vote, but there were a few men—no women at all—and they were sure to vote the way the whites wanted. Now I paid that law-required poll tax from the time I was twenty-one years old in 1937. I married at eighteen but had to wait until I was twenty-one to pay and I paid until the Voting Rights Act of 1965 did away with it. The only thing that I was able to vote for was the trustee of the all-black Harmony School. Back then, local trustees operated every school in the county, and we had three at Harmony. They did the hiring, and they looked out for everything at the school. They didn't get no pay. They just was over the school. And this election would come once a year, like the first Saturday in March you would have a new trustee vote, and they would rotate, so every three years a trustee's time would end out. You'd have to have your poll tax paid up to vote in that one election, which wasn't nothing. We didn't even need a poll tax receipt to vote for that local trustee.

Now, whenever I started trying to register for real voting, I must have been in my upper twenties. But when I'd go in to register at the courthouse in Carthage, they would say, "We're not registering any more, the books are closed," or "the board got the books today." The message was that I need not go back. We didn't go in so regular then, because we knowed that they wasn't going to take on no new registers, especially us. But we started again around 1959, and after we got with the NAACP and Medgar Evers came up to Harmony, we really started again, and sometimes we just did it for the heck of it. Go in and say, "When can we register?" Finally they started letting some of us register, but when you'd go in, you had to do this long literacy test, and you'd know you couldn't pass, because that test was very complicated. They asked you all these questions. Then they gave you an article in the Mississippi constitution. I had to copy it down, just like in the book, which took a whole sheet of paper. Then you had to interpret it and tell what it means—and even a lawyer could not interpret what that was about. So we just kept going in and going in. Dovie and me, every time we'd go to town, we'd try to register, and fill out these long sheets and stand there and stand there. When we'd go back, they'd say, "The board said you didn't pass the test," and every now and then we'd ask, "What board?" Said, "We've got a board that decides on when you'll vote and how you'll vote."

Then one day in 1961, me and Dovie decided we'd just go in. We was in town doing something, and I said, "Let's go up and try to register." We was in the old truck and Cleo was with us. We went in on the south side of the courthouse where the registrar's office was, started up the steps, and Cleo followed us but stopped on the outside, down in front of the courthouse. Me and Dovie went stepping on up and went in the courthouse. We looked down the hall at the registrar's office, and I told Dovie, "Well, they got us. They got us today." And looked like to me it was about ten or twelve men there, chewing tobacco. Had on red flannel shirts and overalls, some of 'em, and some in khaki suits. I said, "We can't turn around and go back. If we start running, we'll keep on running." And Dovie said, "No we can't run. We're going to have to go on." There was a sign just as we came in said, "Colored women go downstairs to the back"—to the black women's restroom. Back then it was white and black restrooms—"White Only," and "Negroes" or "Colored Only." Me and Dovie went downstairs and Dovie prayed. She said, "Lord, must we go? Show it to us. Must we go?" And I said, "Dovie, we're going to have to go." Dovie was praying, and she said, "Let's go. God's got a shield over us, so they can't touch us."

Then Dovie walked up those steep stairways coming out of the basement, coming like we're going to fight in a war—stepping up them steps and starting down the hall, not knowing whether we was going to be cut down or let go. We walked down the hall, they was standing all around and the circuit clerk was just clustered with 'em, like they had us blocked off. To get in the office, we just had to rub right up among 'em, touch 'em, and walk right in by 'em. They couldn't stand to look us in the face, turned their heads away, and when we passed, they said, "it's a bunch of goddamn, stinking billy goats," and we marched through there, "Excuse me. Excuse me." They thought they was going to get us cut off from each other, but they didn't. We walked right on in to the circuit clerk's office, and told 'em, "We want to register today." He gave us this literacy test, and we copied it down, and we stood there with our backs to the men, waiting for any minute for those Klansmen to come and hit us over the head or knock us down. But they didn't. They didn't bother us like that. But they did come in while we registered, and put a card down beside each of us there from the back of us. We didn't even know who it was. And I looked at the card, and read it. It was just a little card, but it had two big red eyes on it, and it said, "The eyes of the

5. Leake County Courthouse, in Carthage, where Winson and her sister Dovie tried to register to vote since the 1930s and were finally successful in 1962. Personal collection of Jewell Dassance.

Klan's upon you. You have been identified by the White Knights of the Ku Klux Klan." And I picked it up and looked at it, and I handed it to the circuit clerk, and I said, "Look here. What is this?" He said, "I don't know. I ain't got nothing to do with that." He was almost trembling. He was scared to death. We stood and we filled out the literacy test, and explained it the best we could. We just said something, 'cause there wasn't no way you could explain it, and then we walked out.

And when we came back downstairs and went out, Cleo was standing down in front of the courthouse. He was looking so strange with his eyes—hands folded, and we saw some man—I knew him well, 'cause he was one of the head leaders in the Klan. He was standing off from Cleo and looking like he was cursing him. I said, "What's happening to Cleo?" Me and Dovie rushed down the stairs and asked Cleo what had happened. He said, "I haven't done anything. I was just standing up here by this car, and that man came up and started cursing and told me I was leaning on this car and told me to get and kept cursing me out." So we went on around on the side of the Power Company where our truck was and went home.

There was a few more in our little group that had tried to register. But mostly everybody had given up, because the Klan had done got pretty rough. But me and Dovie and our sister, Alice, and a few more of us strong with the NAACP would go in. Now Murray McDonald was one of us that had registered successfully. He and my husband was on the registrar's book, but even that didn't mean you could vote. Folks were afraid unless you had some whites that would back you up, because they had to be sure you were voting in their favor. If they needed your vote, then they wanted you to vote. All the while we were getting real, real mad and kept doing things for the heck of it. So we kept going to NAACP meetings and telling about how we was being harassed, and testifying about the bad voting problems for black people in Leake County, and we were reporting to the U. S. Commission on Civil Rights, and finally, in 1962, the Justice Department sent down lawyers Bob Owen and Frank Schwelb. We met with them several times and after that Frank met with the circuit clerk and some other officials in Carthage. Then, Frank told us to go and try to register again. We went and there wasn't no Klansmen around, and this time, the circuit clerk gave us the form about interpreting an article of the constitution, and I wrote down the article that he gave me, and then when it came to interpret it, I said, "It said what it meant, and it meant what it said." The next day I went back and they told me, "Winson, you passed," and Dovie passed too.

Then through the NAACP we got exposed to the outside world and got in touch with Vernon Jordan, the director of the Voter Education Project in Atlanta, and we got little grants from him to start our own voter registration project. He would send us like $150 and we would give it to four or five people to get them to bring somebody to register, and when we used up the money we would send vouchers and get a little bit more. But I stood on that courthouse square and grabbed people and carried them in and they would be mad but they hated to argue. "Come on in. You ain't in no trouble," and we'd carry 'em in. And different ones like from our church was pretty brave, and one or two from over at Ofahoma and Lena would bring some in. But right here in Harmony community, it was the best of all.

When the Voting Rights Act passed in 1965, we felt a new day had come. We got a batch of money—like $700—from Vernon Jordan, and we scattered money all over the county. People brought folks to the courthouse and then there'd be somebody to carry 'em in, or somebody else would catch people on the street and drag them in, and we registered over 500 people in one year. After the Justice Department started coming and the Voting Rights Act and our voter registration project started, the circuit clerk was too afraid to do too much. We carried in a lot of Choctaw Indians too and they gave us good support for a long time, because we had to help the Indians here in Leake County with food, and clothes, and with their legal problems. They had just as many problems as we had back then, and they didn't have no help at all.

Of course, after registering people, you always had to stay after 'em to push 'em to vote, and one thing for sure—who plain didn't register or vote, was people working for white people. The easiest folks to get to help us and to register were the farmers. At that time, farming was going out of business, and people didn't have nothing to lose and were glad to get that little money to help carry people around. They would bring 'em to the back of what used to be a Chevrolet place where black folks congregated. If federal observers or people coming to register were looking for me, I would wear a red dress. I told them, "You can't miss me." Then we'd take a little stroll, and go from there on up through town to the courthouse—always mostly rural people, and non-professionals, and non-business folks. Business people didn't support us, even the few we had at the time. Some people would lay you out. One lady on the street just cursed us. "You don't get me into a mess. I can register if I want to. You don't have to carry me nowhere." And one man said to me, "A woman—you're out of a woman's place. You ought to go somewhere and sit down. If you'd get out of the way, the men could handle things. You women are in the way." And that's what we had to go through—criticizing by the men, some of the professional people calling us cowards, and making fun of us. Those very people—some stopped coming to our church, and one man moved his letter from the church to keep from being with us. It was rough—I couldn't blame nobody. Because like Medgar always told us, "If you don't have nothing to give 'em, don't worry. They'll come in one day. But in the meantime, you got a job on your hands, and just tell 'em to get out of your way." But they wouldn't leave us alone, see. Things would be going pretty good, and we had the white community kind of shook up, and then here come some black folks telling us, "You need to do this, and you need to do that." But, we knew what we was doing, and on through the years, when we made a move, being with the NAACP and being out there for so long, we knew what we needed. And it's still the same today—don't need people advising us on what to do or not do. They need to get involved and attend meetings, and then they'll know whether we're right or wrong.

Chapter Three

"I'M READY TO GO": SCHOOL DESEGREGATION

In 1954, the Supreme Court unanimously ruled in Brown v. the Board of Education *that segregated schools were unconstitutional. While this was a victory for African Americans, the white resistance intensified throughout the South. The fears and threat of education for black people was even stronger than the fear of their voting and political empowerment. Visions of miscegenation and specters of "race-mixing" at a young age, particularly for their white daughters, raised resistance to a fever pitch. Also, education for blacks had always meant the possible loss of workers and posed a terrible threat to the economy. As Governor James Vardaman put it in 1899, "The Negro is not permitted to advance and their education only spoils a good field hand—it is money thrown away." At the local and state levels, white politicians declared "never" to their constituencies, and vowed to thwart the federal government's interference in their "way of life." In Mississippi, two months after the decision, the segregationist Citizens' Council was organized in the Delta, and later that year, Tom Brady, a judge from Brookhaven, Mississippi, gave an incendiary speech titled "Black Monday" that espoused segregationist ideology in full detail. Also in 1954, the Mississippi state legislature passed and voters approved an amendment to the state constitution to abolish compulsory school attendance. Because Southern states refused to comply with the original* Brown *ruling, the Supreme Court later issued a second opinion,* Brown II, *which mandated schools to desegregate "with all deliberate speed."*

By 1956, the Mississippi legislature passed additional laws designed to circumvent the court ruling, and that same year, the State Sovereignty Commission was established to preserve segregation at all costs. The commission, which was state-funded, investigated persons who were believed to be subversive or a threat to the status quo. Meanwhile, violence and other attacks on African Americans intensified. Notably, in 1955, several black men were murdered, including fourteen-year-old Emmett Till and Reverend George Lee. Lee was a leader in the Belzoni, Mississippi, chapter of the NAACP, while young Emmett Till had been murdered for allegedly whistling at a white woman.

In response to the Brown *decision, the Leake County School Board came up with a plan to defy the desegregation order by agreeing to build new schools for blacks. The plan called for Jordan High School, Greer High, and Murphy High to be built in three towns near Harmony, and they were later named after their black principals. There was never any consideration of preserving the Harmony School and sending white children there, if indeed the school board was forced to come up with a desegregation plan. Realizing this attempt on the part of the all-white school board to sidestep desegregation, Harmony School trustees began meeting with the Leake County School Board in opposition to the new schools. The community of Harmony knew that the board would eventually want to close the Harmony School, which had functioned so successfully in educating young black children in the years preceding* Brown. *After being challenged by the Harmony trustees, the school board agreed to put an eighth-grade school in Harmony and in Lena, another small community. Blacks saw it as another attempt to appease them, and as the sixties approached, the loss of the Harmony School appeared inevitable. Winson and others appealed for help to Medgar Evers, Mississippi Field Secretary for the NAACP, based in Jackson. Always ready to be on the road and helping community efforts, he was a shining inspiration until his assassination in 1963. Winson and others throughout the state came to love and respect him. Evers suggested that Harmony leaders direct their efforts toward desegregation, and in 1961, a suit calling for countywide school desegregation was filed—the first suit against a rural school system in Mississippi, with Diane Hudson, Dovie's daughter, as plaintiff.*

After prolonged legal processes, in February 1964, the Fifth Circuit Court of Appeals in Diane Hudson, et al., *v.* Leake County, et al. *ordered the county to submit desegregation plans by July 1964. The county complied by agreeing to desegregate the schools beginning at the first-grade level the first year, and then to add grades each year thereafter. In the meantime, plans were made to open a private academy for the "white flight" from the public schools. This happened all over the state of Mississippi when desegregation became a reality, and many of the academies still exist today. Thus, the public schools are majority black, indicating the rising tide of resegregation.*

Because the Leake County court order called for first-grade desegregation in September 1964, Diane Hudson, in high school, was not eligible, but A. J. and Minnie Lewis were willing to send their first-grader, Debra, to the elementary school. The days leading to the school's opening were filled with tension and fear, and the black community had no idea of possible white reaction. The bodies of the three murdered civil rights workers had just been found in neighboring Neshoba County, and the white community was still angered by the Freedom Summer volunteers who had been working in the county since June. John Doar, first assistant, Civil Rights Division of the Justice Department, and his staff were in and out of the county all summer, aware of the potential for violence, but determined to uphold the law. Doar was known for his fearlessness in going to trouble spots all during the movement. Over twenty federal marshals from outside the state were in the county. Jean Fairfax knew that they were expecting trouble because of the history of Klan bombings and violence in the county, and she recalls seeing tear gas canisters and rifles in the trunk of a federal marshal's car.

The local paper headlines on September 3, 1964, "LONE NEGRO GIRL ENTERS PREVIOUS

WHITE SCHOOL," were followed by a detailed story of Debra Lewis's enrollment, including her arrival with Jean Fairfax and Derrick Bell, in a "light blue late-model automobile." In an accompanying editorial, titled "Let's Get Back to Normal," the first paragraph read, "It's been a tense and disappointing week in the lives of Carthaginians and Leake Countians."

Winson recalls the machinations to close the Harmony School, and the troubles unleashed by the fight to save their school and then to implement school desegregation.

We loved our community and we loved our Harmony School—our big dog Rosenwald School. We always tried to stay here and rely on our own people, even though the men had to go outside the community to work, and we had to go to the bank and to the stores and all. We just stuck together—like when we were losing our school and decided to try and integrate the white school, no other place could have had as much success out in the sticks like us. See, if something is going on, once you come in here, somebody's going to see you, no matter when or where you enter. We had such bad roads so they couldn't just fly in and out like it was a highway. Sometime, when things got rough, the police couldn't even come through here, unless they blowed the siren or blinked their lights. We was just that much together. This community is noted everywhere for taking care of each other. We didn't have no phone, but my husband had an old pickup truck, and others did, and plenty of shotguns. When whites came through here, from Frog Bottom, where we lived, to any border, the Harmony men gave a sign. They'd blow that whistle twice, riding through the community, or else they'd shoot in the air and let 'em know to get on board—someone was coming in. The Klan never did come in here or get out without being marked or being known. The FBI never could find 'em, but we knew who they were. So, we really got mad and rallied together when whites started messing with our Harmony School. All through the years, our people had put a lot into that school. It had started off going through the eighth grade, and then the tenth and then to the twelfth. Our parents believed in children being educated. Now whites had nicer buildings and indoor plumbing and all, but we had the best black school in the county. We had to practice outdoors, but we had the best basketball team in the county. Teachers or parents couldn't make an error, or everyone would be on you, because parents were trustees and they hired and fired. Teachers were the important people back then. When you became a teacher, you had made it, and no one was leaving to go to college or to get jobs—Harmony was our whole world.

After it looked like they were going to close down our school, we made so many trips to the courthouse to try to get the school board to leave Harmony School alone. Even some white citizens supported us and pleaded with the board to leave us alone. Others said that if nobody messed with us, maybe integration wouldn't come. Reverend Morgan Scott, a white minister, went with us to a meeting with the board, and he told them, "Leave those darkies alone—look what is happening in other states just across the line. If you don't leave them alone, you are asking for trouble." The board would not give in. The Harmony community and adjoining white communities signed petitions to save Harmony School and sent it to the school board, and they continued to promise us a good school, but only up through the eighth grade. A beautiful high school was built in Carthage, Jordan High, named after its black principal; then Greer was built in Thomastown and Murphy was built in Walnut Grove, naming them after these black principals they felt could be handled.

Nothing was being done at Harmony, except the school board was slowly taking power away from the Harmony trustees. We continued to have meetings with the board about the need for a school at Harmony. Then they refused to meet any more, and they sent a state representative to explain to us why there would be no school at Harmony. We never accepted their decision. I can hear the sound of the crying even now, on the day trucks backed up to the Harmony school, hauling off things we had raised money for and bought. One Harmony man said he hauled logs eighteen miles on a wagon. Other patrons of the school told about giving cotton to purchase the land for the school. We prayed for righteousness—for some it was like giving the future of our children back into the hands of our slavemasters. Later the school board even took the land and claimed it belonged to them.

Around May 1961, me and Dovie, along with Harmony School trustee Murray McDonald, decided to contact state NAACP Field Secretary Medgar Evers about starting a chapter here and helping us with the Harmony School situation. Medgar Evers was a hero, a smart and kind man, and fearless, and he traveled all over this state to help black people for about nine years until they killed him in 1963. Medgar's coming here brought a lot of division

6. Harmony Vocational High School, 1954. Personal collection of Anita Johnson.

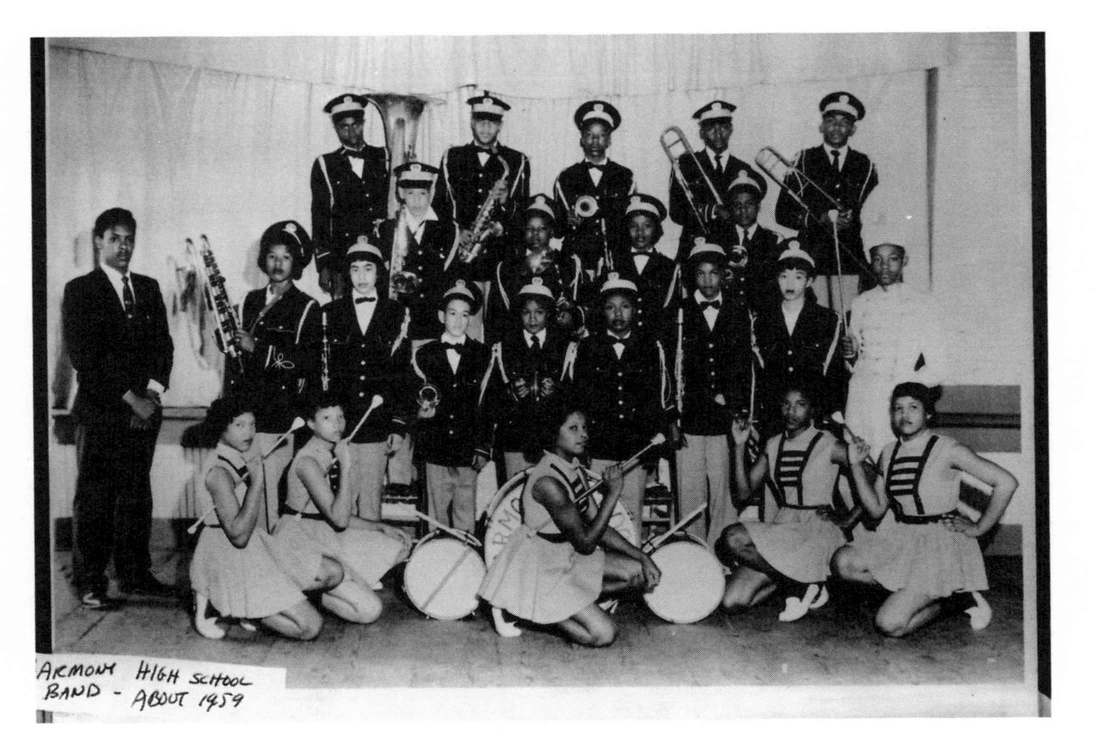

7. Harmony high school band, 1959. Personal collection of Winson Hudson.

within our community. Some of the people were fearful because we all knew that involvement with the NAACP could bring the Klan on them. After a lot of talk, we had Medgar to come out from Jackson and talk with us. The meeting was held at our Galilee Church, and Medgar spoke to a crowded audience. The fear was so great that some of the community did not want him to speak, especially since the deputy sheriff and men he had deputized were there on the scene. Some of our people had snitched about the meeting. One man, Charlie Edward Gates, had invited the deputy and his men in, and they sat on the front pew with their guns showing. It was insulting. They had not been invited. There were feelings of anger, fear, and anxiety among our people. There was raging anger from me and Cleo and Dovie and a couple of others. We resented the deputy sheriff and his henchmen being there, sitting on the front row of our church with guns. Murray and Medgar came to the podium. Voices were heard from the audience saying, "Let him speak. Don't let him speak." Cleo and Murray insisted that Medgar speak, but first, Murray asked the sheriff if he had anything to say. He stood up with his pistol at his side and said, "I am here to protect y'all," and turning to Medgar he said, "The Negroes and whites ain't gonna let what's happened in other states happen here." I will never forget the brave expression on Medgar's face as he rose and addressed the audience and the deputies. He turned to the deputies, smiled, and said, "You are different from most police and sheriffs in other parts of the state, for they are the ones who allow and participate in the cruelty, harassment, and intimidation of the Negroes. I refer you to the Negro lady who said 'I know my place; my place is anywhere my tax dollars go.' My job is to integrate schools! For those of you who feel they can get Harmony School back, go ahead and try it. But, I am with the NAACP and we don't build schools or save schools, we go to the best schools. Schools can be separate but equal, but, here you have three new school buildings, and the education is anything but equal." After Medgar spoke, people was so afraid. Some of 'em sat right in the back and some of 'em got up that night and said, "I will never let my children do this." And, after Medgar spoke a lot of them flew out the door—some slipping out near the end of the meeting to avoid contact with Medgar. Brave men like Murray McDonald, Cleo, and more of our men all gathered around Medgar after the meeting and took him to his car for fear that something bad was going to happen to him.

By the next week, news had spread all around the white community in Leake County that Medgar Evers from the NAACP had been up in Harmony and that the people were trying to send their children to white schools. Some of the white folks even went back to the school board to try and get Harmony School back. After the meeting with Medgar, the school board came out to Galilee Church to explain the benefit of sending Harmony children to Murphy High School over in Walnut Grove. We weren't having it. I told the school board representative, Mr. Ware, "If you don't bring the school back to Harmony, we will be going to your school." He looked at me real angry and said, "Winson, you and your children and your children's children will never live to see that." And one of Governor Ross Barnett's cousins said it would never happen. He said, "Little children's blood will run in the streets like water before [desegregation] will happen in Leake County." He couldn't know that four years later, Leake County would be ordered to integrate its schools, starting with the first grade.

After our first meeting with Medgar, we got back in touch with him and organized the Leake County NAACP in 1961. We got up to fifty members to get our charter. When we would have meetings, there would always be somebody black on the outside snooping around. They'd be watching us all the time. Clara Dotson was the first NAACP president and I was vice-president. Things was really, really rough. Medgar told us from the start that what we were doing was dangerous, and if we didn't have a way to take care of ourselves, we would be pushed out. He said that some of us might even get killed. One of the new NAACP members said, "Won't we be able to get help from the FBI?" And, Medgar said, "The FBI is not on your side." My husband asked, "Well, who can we look to for help?" Medgar said, "Nobody—you all will have to stick together."

One Sunday, a group of us went to Jackson to meet with Constance Baker Motley, attorney for the NAACP from New York. We told her that we came to talk about the school situation in Leake County. She set us up to talk to her co-worker, attorney Derrick Bell from New York, and he told us the white school board would never allow white children to come to our school, no matter how good it was, and the best thing was to file a suit to desegregate the schools in Leake County. At the same time, Dr. Gilbert Mason, the brave NAACP leader from Biloxi, Mississippi, and Medgar from Jackson were in the process of filing desegregation suits. Dr. Mason had even been trying to integrate the beaches down on the coast. We all filed at the same time. Derrick Bell and Constance Baker Motley told us to get fifty-two people to sign petitions, and from that number we would probably only get a few who would go all the way and sign the petitions, since the pressure was so strong. They said that we just couldn't begin with only two or three people because it would be too dangerous. They told us, "Don't force nobody."

We went back home and spread out over the county and got the petitions with fifty-two signatures to desegregate the schools of Leake County. There were only three black lawyers in the state at the time. Two of them, R. Jess Brown and Jack Young, worked with Constance Baker Motley and Derrick Bell to help us. The petition was presented to the school board, and boy, that was the beginning of some rough times.

The local paper came out that Friday and said that Harmony community parents wanted their children to attend white schools. That night, a group of whites came through Harmony, shooting into homes. They wasn't picking certain homes, because they didn't know where the parents lived who was behind the lawsuit. They just came through here and shot in houses on both sides of the road. The next weekend, they came through again and that time, some of Dovie's boys—and some more here—were ready for 'em. The young black men had gotten their guns ready, and they ran the whites out of here. They followed 'em back to their homes and shot into them. This stirred things up so bad that even Governor Ross Barnett came out to Harmony and offered to build a junior college up here. Of course, we didn't believe him and we stayed with the lawsuit.

As we went forward with the case, whites began to put pressure on us. Our petition with the list of names was posted at the courthouse, and the folks who worked for whites or lived on their land were forced to take their names off. Finally, only thirteen names out of fifty-two were left. I was so disappointed. I cried. The names left on the petition were the Hudsons, the Dotsons, and the McDonalds. There were other folks as brave as me and Cleo.

The blacks who were not involved in the school desegregation case would not offer us any help. They would laugh at us and say that we had no business getting into such a mess—that we should have stayed in our place. Around this same time, I had gotten in a bit of other trouble after I wrote a twenty-two-page letter to two black men in Congress, Adam Clayton Powell from New York and Charles Diggs from Michigan, telling them about the problems we were having getting Farmer's Home Administration (FHA) loans. Black folks couldn't get no housing, no loans, and no nothing. Local blacks had tried to get loans and they were always turned down, and it got worse after the school suit started. When I wrote the letter to the congressmen, I told them that only a very few blacks were able to get the kind of loans they wanted and that white folks were always getting loans to build large chicken houses and to buy cows. A few blacks who were loyal to the whites were able to buy land and cows, but most of us couldn't get a loan. It was a bad time when some black people thought we were crazy and white people would deprive of us loans, credit, and everything to keep down the push for civil rights.

I learned about the congressmen through the NAACP and Medgar Evers, and in my letter to them I wrote, "We have a 60-acre farm and we are going to have to give it up because we cannot get a loan to operate it." To make sure that the congressmen got these letters, I had to wrap 'em in a socks box and send them to my husband's brother in Chicago like it was a gift. See, our mail was being opened down here. I sent two or three letters by my brother-in-law to different places. I just kept the letters going—something going somewhere. We had the mail investigated, too. We had so much missing mail that we started sending it to Jackson by Behonor McDonald's daughter and our pastor. They'd come out here to visit, and we'd give 'em mail and let 'em drop it in the box in Jackson. But when folks would write back, we'd still be in danger.

In two weeks, I got a letter back from Congressman Diggs saying that he had received my letter and had circulated it around the White House. It had also been given to the secretary of the Department of Agriculture, Orville Freeman. In the next day or so, I had a letter back from Orville Freeman. He said that he had written to Charlton Phillips, supervisor of the Leake County Farmer's Home Administration, telling him to take a look at our farm and see what he could do for us. Phillips sent us a letter to come in, and me and Cleo went down to the courthouse where the local FHA office was located. We walked upstairs and sat down in the waiting room. Phillips walked out and said, "Come in Cleo and Winson." He went in the drawer and got the letter that he had received from Orville Freeman. He said, "Listen, I want y'all to know one damn thing—I run this county and damn niggers in Harmony will not run it. Y'all need to get jobs and go to work. You niggers think you can live and not work." But, we was working hard—didn't have nothing to work with—with no money, no way to make no money. He had told Dovie to "go to Chicago, like all the rest of 'em—to send her boys to Chicago and get a job." He told us, "If you get any money from the FHA, you will have to deal with me. Do y'all understand?" We said, "Yes, we understand." We left. We knew then that even more pressure would be placed on us. We were so humiliated that we did not tell anybody what had happened. This business with the FHA had gotten me and Cleo both in trouble, and we could have been killed about that, and we were already in deep with the school suit.

Things got worse as we stayed with the desegregation suit at the same time. A local friend who was always with us, Willie Earl Lewis, had lived on the same farm all of his life. His father had raised his family there. But when Willie's name came out on that petition, he was ordered to take it off. He refused and the white folks forced him off their land. He was so angry he enrolled his three children a few years later in the white school in Madden, but the following year they made that school into the private academy, and he decided to send them to the public schools in Carthage. Willie bought a little farm where he still lives today. Some of the other folks on the school petition were employed by Presto Manufacturing Company in Jackson and whites tried to get them fired over there. But the company management was located up North and when it found out, they told the folks in Jackson they had better leave our folks alone.

When the lawsuit was filed and the court case got underway in 1961, the plaintiff was Diane Hudson, my sister's daughter. Dovie knew no fear, but with the filing of the school desegregation suit, more and more pressure was put on her. They threatened to take her land. The case had gotten national attention by now, and then a conference was held at Mt. Beulah to bring in people from around the country to hear about what was going on in Mississippi. Dovie went down there with Jean Fairfax, who was helping us and who worked with the American Friends Service Committee. Dovie told Jean about how they was trying to foreclose on her and that she had eight children still at home and was about to lose her land. Jean got the American Friends Service Committee to send Dovie a check, but the bank refused to cash it. Dovie took it to Morris Warwick, the man she owed for the land and he finally gave her a receipt that the land had been paid for in full.

We knew we could be blown away any time by then. Medgar was so concerned about us because we was in the middle of Klan country. Other people was catching it too. Some of the people on the petition had their own incomes, but me and Cleo and Dovie had nothing but our land. Me and Cleo had applied for loans, but they turned us down over and over, since I was president of the NAACP by now. We rented land from the whites because we couldn't get enough money to make ends meet. We grew corn for cattle feed and we grew our own food: peanuts, vegetables, and sugar cane. We had already borrowed money from the bank to pay for fertilizer, supplies, and a few clothes. But, when this suit came, all of our credit was cut off. The blacks turned on us. We couldn't get help from them. We were cut loose from everything and we could no longer rent the land. Me and Cleo had an old pickup truck. Me, him, and Dovie went all over trying to borrow money on it. Finally, we heard about a black credit union in Yazoo City that was a long way from Harmony. We got in that truck and headed to Yazoo City and we were able to get $125 and Dovie got $75.

A lot of blacks were afraid of us, but we knew our little group had to stick together and get out and hustle. Sometimes we felt so alone. A few of the blacks who were not afraid would give Dovie's boys day work. We got enough money to buy a power saw and we took that saw and the old truck and we started cutting wood all across the county. Me and Dovie's second-oldest boy, Glover, would cut wood and

Cleo would haul it. I wore men's clothes, overalls, and shirts and I could saw as much wood as any man. And this timber helped us to survive these hard times.

So, we were starting to get known by the whites as having lawyers and Washington people on our side, and next time we tried to apply for a loan and went in to see Charlton Phillips with the local FHA, things was different. He took us right on in this time, and I never want to be treated any nicer. We sat there a half-day filling out loan papers to get things that we needed—twelve milk cows, money to buy fertilizer and seed for our pasture, money to clean up land to plant grass, and a small amount to renovate our house. We did not borrow up to our limit because we thought that they would foreclose on us. After this, we were able to get more loans. Mr. Phillips was feeling the pressure by then from the national FHA office because we kept complaining to Washington and they investigated every two or three months. Other black folks started coming around to ask us about loans, and we sent them into the FHA office in Carthage, or I took 'em myself and helped 'em fill out applications and they were able to get loans.

But one problem we had with the FHA was that, for black people, they would finance old houses not wanted by the whites. They were old board houses that did not hold up to the weather. When they were bought, these houses would be moved onto black property. We filed a complaint about that too and put a stop to it. There was not a single brick home in the county at this time that belonged to blacks.

Still the hard times came in 1963 and 1964, as the school desegregation suit went on. I remember going so many times into that federal courthouse in Jackson and seeing big pictures that covered a whole wall around it. There were pictures of black folks picking cotton, women dragging cotton sacks and down on their knees picking cotton, and having the sacks weighed in. And, then there was a picture of Ole Missy sitting there on the porch. We had to sit and look at those pictures through it all, and the sad thing about it was that Medgar was so blue. Once during that lawsuit at the Jackson courthouse the bathrooms was locked up, so we couldn't use them. Medgar went to the judge to ask him to open them up and they was mad, didn't want to open 'em up. What did they think we was going to do? Just sit there all day long? And Medgar would stand with his hands folded, saying over and over, "This is not the end. This is not the end."

Medgar would always try to help us—we loved him. He said, "Well, you got the lawsuit going for you and you are going to win out. Somebody'll go after a while. Don't worry about it." My sister Dovie said, "Medgar, I'm going to stay here and pay the cost, no matter what it is." Everybody loved Medgar. When he was assassinated in 1963, we didn't care any more what happened. Behonor McDonald heard it on the radio and came to tell us. We were so angry. We just walked the roads and hollered and cried and cried and hollered. Then we met in my house, and we felt like just taking guns and shooting up everything. I was nonviolent, but my husband was not. He always said if he got killed, he was taking someone with him.

Finally, in 1964, three years from when that suit that Medgar filed for Jackson, and Dr. Gilbert Mason filed for Biloxi, and we filed for Leake County, that judge ordered the schools desegregated, one grade at a time, starting in the fall of 1964 with the first grade. So, next came the countdown to D-Day or desegregation day, and our first job was to find parents with kids about to enter school—like six-year-old first-graders. Well now, though Dovie had been the main plaintiff [in Diane's name], Diane was in high school and Dovie didn't have a first-grader. We went everywhere trying to find somebody to go to the white school. We knew what the pressure would be like because we had already gone through bombings, shootings, and foreclosures, losing jobs and such. Me, Jean Fairfax from the American Friends Service Committee, Benny Bounds from Carthage, and Dovie was going way out into the west part of the county trying to find parents who would be willing to send their first-graders to school. We held meetings to talk to parents. My husband, Cleo, worked really hard.

After the court decision, there were people coming by fairly regularly from the Department of Justice, but we didn't have no confidence in those people. This was all prior to the opening of school in early September, and by mid-August, we had about six children willing to go whose parents had signed the petition. Other parents were still scared because it was really dangerous. Somebody would have to carry these children to school from Harmony, way out in the rural—thirteen miles to Carthage—and bring 'em back, and didn't nobody have no big cars. We just had old pickups that broke down all the time. The men who might have carried the children was working at Presto in Jackson and couldn't do it.

Finally, at one of our meetings, Benny Bounds said "Mrs. Hudson, I got somebody that I know will send their child to the school. A. J. Lewis has a daughter, Debra." Next day, I went and found them. A. J. and Minnie, his wife, were staying with Minnie's mother. I talked to A. J. and he said, "Yeah, we'll let Debra go." No idea that she'd be able, but they were willing, and I saw A. J. was strong.

The last few days before school opened white people were riding by day and night, threatening everyone. One man had a gin and he furnished black folk fertilizer, seed, and everything it took to make a crop. He was one of the main ones riding by and threatening to cut loose against black people all over the county: "If you take part in this, then I want the money you owe me and you won't get anything more." He had a lot of people tied up with land, and supplies and stock, through loans to black farmers and the notes he held against them. It was terrible—all this coming down to D-Day—desegregation day.

That weekend before the schools opened, John Doar and other people from the Justice Department were here and FBI people who had on white shirts and black ties, but they had their coats off and they were just as dusty as could be with this clay dust and their shirts sticking to 'em. And everyone running around and passing in cars and it was so tense. We were just wondering was we going to get blowed off the map.

I can remember that first day—it was the Tuesday after the Labor Day weekend, when the schools opened. Jean Fairfax from the American Friends Service Committee was there along with NAACP attorney Derrick Bell. Federal marshals were there—sitting there looking. We had all gathered at Debra's house out on the porch. Jean Fairfax was standing in the front yard talking to Debra. And we was all in tears, some on the porch and some inside, so sad, just wondering what was going to happen. And, after a while, Debra said, "What's everybody waiting for? I'm ready to go."

They had all the streets blocked off there around the house, down Cotton Boulevard and all around. Jean Fairfax and Derrick Bell and Minnie Lewis went with Debra—they had the route all mapped out—knew exactly how many minutes it would take to go up there and register and come back. Minnie walked Debra into the school and Jean and Derrick waited at the car, and they stayed and stayed, and we was just ready to start screaming. We didn't hear nothing like bombs or shooting or nothing. But they all came back and everything went okay.

Now they sat Debra in the back of the room at the beginning and they had talked about moving her around to different rooms, but she happened to get a pretty good teacher, and that teacher—I've always wanted to thank her. She told the school people that Debra was her student and would be treated like all the others. You'd ask Debra how she was doing, and she'd say "I'm all right." So they at least wasn't jumping on her and harassing her, like they did the older ones when they went the next year. Debra went right on ahead and finished high school at Leake County High and it never seemed to have any bad effects on her.

After Debra enrolled, that family really suffered. It was what happened to black people fighting for their rights. A. J., the father, lost his job, and somebody tried to burn their house up, and a black man jumped on him and beat him up in Carthage. A. J. was just walking on the street and they didn't have no argument or nothing—just jumped on him. And that same man came over here to a ball game we was having, and said he'd come to beat Cleo up or hurt him some way, but we got wind of it and he was run off right away.

Then, my brother, Glover, let A. J. and Minnie have two-and-a-half acres of land real cheap because they couldn't find any place to live. And they was able to get an FHA loan for a house because of all the work we had done, and the American Friends Service Committee helped too. There were a few problems—had to build a septic tank 'cause they couldn't get a sewage tank from the city—but at least they were able to stay in the county.

None of the bad things happening to A. J. surprised us because before we even won the lawsuit, thirteen teachers were fired at one time. Half of 'em had to leave the county—good teachers—just because they had some connection to us and to the NAACP. Any association with the NAACP at that time meant you could lose your job. Medgar had warned us, "Tell those teachers to stay away from you. If you don't have a job for 'em, don't fool 'em, because they will lose their jobs, and they won't get a recommendation for another one." And that's exactly what happened. Then, the school board started making black principals and teachers list all the organizations they belonged to. They even had the teachers sign the statement, and they had a notary to sign it at faculty meetings at each school.

I warned Mary Gates, one of the teachers and a good friend, and her husband not to talk to me or Dovie or to have anything to do with us, because we knew what would happen to her. But Mary continued to give small donations to the NAACP and to talk to us. At the end of the 1963 school year, her principal notified her that she would not be hired the next year and that her husband was being transferred to another high school. When they asked the superintendent he told her that she would have to come to the next school board meeting and tell them that she was not a member of the NAACP and did not believe in it or participate in it. Mary said she would go to the meeting and tell them that "all blacks who are not already members should join the NAACP." He told her right then that she was fired, and her own black principal told her she would never work in Leake County again. But Mary was fearless and told that principal that there were eighty-one other counties and forty-nine other states where she could work. Later she and her husband worked in the all-black town of Mound Bayou, but years later we got them back here. The NAACP told the school superintendent that we would get him re-elected if he would bring them home, and he did, and Mary is head of our NAACP right now.

A lot of our people suffered even if they weren't directly involved during all of this. Whites wanted to frighten the community and did a good job. You know we'd walk down the street in Carthage and you'd meet a black person going to borrow money, or especially a teacher—they'd see you coming, they'd turn back. Some of 'em even ran from us. They laugh about it now. One man laughs and says, "Well, I made a lot of steps running from you all in Carthage. I'd duck in a store when I saw you coming—playing like I had business—and even buying something I didn't want—just to dodge you." But see, I didn't blame him. It was a lonesome time, I tell you, a lonesome time. Except for our own Galilee Church, wouldn't none of 'em welcome us. You'd go to the churches, and I would just stand and have to steal a sermon, 'cause the ministers wanted us to go away, and I don't see why—they didn't have nothing to lose. The congregation was supporting them, but I would go, and I would just stand up in the church and make a little speech. And the minister wouldn't say nothing. He'd just dismiss the congregation.

Later on Dovie's house was bombed twice. Our house was meant to be bombed, but we heard the truck. I was night watching until twelve that night and the Klan was backing into our driveway. My daughter, Annie Maude, was living with us while her husband was in Vietnam. She was expecting a baby and was so sick that night and she heard the truck too. I told her to get up and rush into the back room. My husband and I got ready to start shooting, but by this time, the German shepherd dog had forced the Klan to move on. I ran to the phone to call Dovie to be ready. By this time, a bomb went off at her house and I heard my sister's baby girl, Mary, screaming. I started outside and Cleo was shooting, emptying every gun. Annie Maude was running to me, thinking the Klan might kill me. She didn't understand all the shooting and bombing. I pulled aloose from her and she fell on the concrete porch. When I came to myself, I heard my daughter say, "Mama, I am hurt." Next day, we rushed her to the Hinds General Hospital. The baby had to come. The baby was saved but had to stay in the hospital for a long time. That was my first grandson, Donovan.

Donovan was so little, and when we came home, we thought he would die, and I stayed close to Annie Maude and the baby all of the time. He was so beautiful and Cleo was so proud to have a grandson. We called the hospital three or four times a day, and after three weeks we took him to Jackson for a checkup. It was this beautiful clinic and the receptionist carried us down the hall to a little room with concrete floors, no rugs, and mops and brooms and cleaning supplies stored right next to us. An older black lady and retired teacher was waiting there to see a doctor. I got so mad and asked her if she sat there all the time, and she said yes—that it was the place colored people sat. I told Annie Maude that I would not let her and Donovan sit back there. She started pleading, "Mama please, I have gone through enough. They might do something to my baby. Don't go up there. You're gonna have them kill my baby." I told her she better go on and leave and take the baby because he would not be seeing a doctor back there. When Annie Maude couldn't stop me, she got her bag, wrapped up the baby, and

8. Winson and Dovie Hudson, 1975. Personal collection of Winson Hudson.

went to the car. I went up where the whites were sitting and the receptionist came over and said the doctor would be with Annie and the baby soon. I said, "I want to see the doctor at once." He came out and asked what he could do for me. I asked, "Why does my grandson have to go down this hall into a cold room with cleaning supplies? Do you know this baby's daddy is in Vietnam and has been hit three times?" He wouldn't look at me, but said, "I didn't tell you to go back there," but I told him his receptionist took us back there and he knew the system. He said to get the baby and he would see him right away, but I told him no and that we wouldn't be back. We went straight to the NAACP office in Jackson and the director, Alex Waites, made notes to file a complaint and directed us to another doctor. In about thirty days, the first doctor sent us a bill. We ignored it and the secretary called. I told her to "forget it. Now sue me," and I hung up on her. I never heard from them again.

It was about a month before the bombing when we came home a Sunday evening and found Annie Maude crying. The sheriff had brought her a telegram saying her husband had been injured in Vietnam. He was guarding the Cambodian border for the army the night they tried to destroy our home in the U.S.A. He was hit three times, in his leg, his knee, and his chest, and the bullet in his chest will have to stay there as long as he lives. We didn't write him about the house bombings, but he learned about it, and we wondered how he felt about this country that his son would have to grow up in.

Chapter Four

FREEDOM SUMMER AND "GOOD THINGS": CIVIL RIGHTS MOVEMENT, 1960–1970

"Risking everything for change, ordinary black Mississippians led the way by daring to attack from within the beast of white supremacy, segregation and discrimination. Plantation worker, student, maid, the employed and the unemployed, joined with civil rights workers from inside and outside the state in a great struggle for freedom—to continue the struggle that began when the first African slaves looked out from the auction block at this strange and faraway land." These words are from the brochure inviting people to the 1994 celebration of Freedom Summer, which had been held thirty years earlier in Mississippi. In the early sixties, the various civil rights groups working in Mississippi formed the Council of Federated Organizations (COFO) and set the course of Freedom Summer. It changed Mississippi forever.

The plan was to bring black and white students as summer volunteers in various communities to work along with local groups. They established freedom schools, which introduced black history for the first time to many children, voter and citizenship education projects informed local people of their right to vote and of federal programs available to them, and they performed other tasks, based on the needs of the community where the workers were assigned. In June, at the very beginning of the project, three of the workers, Michael Schwerner, James Chaney, and Andrew Goodman, were murdered in Neshoba County, about thirteen miles from Harmony. Tension was always present and overt opposition began early in Harmony when the county, claiming that the property belonged to them, flatly refused to let the workers set up shop in the buildings of the old Harmony School. (In 1969, the community bought back and regained control over the historic buildings and land.)

Many of the volunteers also worked to organize at the precinct and county levels toward sending a mostly black delegation, representing the Mississippi Freedom Democratic Party (MFDP), to the 1964 National Democratic Convention in Atlantic City. Movement leaders founded the MFDP in the spring of 1964, to establish an independent grassroots political party. An immediate goal was to challenge the regular state Democratic Party's delegation at the national convention in August. The hope was that part or all of the MFDP delegation would be seated, demonstrating the true nature of the voting population in Mississippi. Summer workers were invaluable in this work of political education and organizing. There were approximately thirty-three communities in Mississippi with Freedom Summer projects, and Harmony was one of them.

Jane Adams, a white student from Illinois, was one of the summer volunteers in Harmony. Adams lived with Dovie Hudson and kept a detailed journal on her life and work that summer. Her insights, along with Winson's memories, give not only a picture of the problems and intimidation the community faced but also the positive impact of Freedom Summer, which lasted far beyond the three months of summer and forged relationships that still exist today.

FROM JANE ADAMS' JOURNAL:

July 7, 1964, 6 P.M. Went to Winson and Cleo Hudson's house, helped (sort of) milk the cows, rode the horse, got some more information on the administration of federal funds from Mr. Hudson, got ride home on passing truck at dark. Picked up a partially blind man who lives in a shack just up the road from us. Trucks run a free taxi service here, as do cars. 8 P.M. Read about federal programs, took bath outside by spigot—nude in the night, Peggy giggling as Carole and I stood bare to the stars and pigs and trees, and I got clean. 11 P.M. to bed.

July 8: Things are really great here. We do face great hostility from the white community, but at least for this summer I don't think we face any real violence. A cross was put up by the store and charred, but the people didn't stay long enough to get it burning well. The sheriff heard of it and came to see about it a couple of days later. Tacks were strewn on the road late one night. The whole community was tense the weekend of July 4th. Everyone here is armed, but it is a tension of caution, not of fear. One cuts the lights when a car goes by, looks out cautiously and everyone else keeps dancing. We don't travel at all after dark if it can be avoided. But the whites know the FBI is all over; Navy teams are scouring the area [for the bodies of Schwerner, Chaney, and Goodman].

It's strange how one adjusts a mind-set to existing circumstances—we almost never go into town, and when we do, two or three people always stay together. We never travel alone. We always tell someone where we are going, even to the outhouse; we watch for cars full of white people and notice frequency of passage and take tag numbers, yet all these things quickly become habit and don't interfere in the slightest with work or play.

So let me describe this community. It is such a great place. The roads are red clay with gravel which sinks through, so after heavy rains, they are almost impassible. They wind around the ridges so that one can see miles across woods and scrub and rough pasture and cotton and beans or peas. Houses dotted around generally on the ridge. Many of the houses are quite new and in quite good condition, though the Negro homes have an often-unfinished look about them. FHA or VA loans didn't come through or were less than requested. A good many tarpaper shacks. Harmony community is all Negro. The people own their own land—sixty acres is a good-sized farm. The land is not fully utilized, as clearing takes money, but it is extremely beautiful country. The people too are wonderful—those of Harmony. Warm, friendly, none of the hostilities one finds among many urban Negroes and very little kow-towing. There are apparently a good many who are afraid of us, but they are beginning to lose their fear, as they see things are going well. July 4th there was a big ball game in the field across from the store, with the Choctaws from Neshoba County and people from Midway who are, I think, sharecroppers. About four P.M., some of us began singing freedom songs and gradually more and more adults drifted over and by the time we sang, "We Shall Overcome," we had a huge circle. A good many didn't come, but that's ok. The Choctaws seemed interested in the Freedom School, as did people from Carthage and Midway, so our influence is spreading.

July 9: We went to see the librarian in the Carthage Public Library. She said she knew who we were and that the good people were horrified by the disappearance of the freedom workers in Neshoba County. She prayed every night that the three would turn up alive. The schools should integrate—better schools. Her husband had been a teacher at the Choctaw School. They now have a new school—the best in the county. Went to the courthouse to call Mother. Met Jack who had registered with the police and done laundry. People hurrying by us head down and a youngster of sixteen or so shook his finger at us. Went back to the store in Harmony, typed up housing and canvassing lists, wrote letters for literature to be sent from various Washington agencies. People played cards, listened to records, shelled peas. Watched the "Lone Ranger" for the first time in years. 11:30 to bed.

July 19: Dovie told us stories this morning. "Some years ago two black boys who white people said had been messing with a white lady—they tied 'em behind a car and dragged them up and down the road of the town with their parents standing there watching. And then they burned them boys. That's how they is, for nothing. It's pitiful. I couldn't do an animal that way." Singing this morning, just with the family. "Oh, Freedom," "Come By Here," "I'm Gonna Sit at the

Welcome Table," "Hold On," "Michael Row the Boat Ashore," "Go Tell It on the Mountain," "I'm so Glad I'm Not an Uncle Tom," "Fighting to be Free." Then everybody out to canvass.

July 24: We sent a letter today to Sheriff Russell Edwards from the Leake County Movement, with copies to the Mayor, chief of police, Americans for the Preservation of the White Race, the newspaper, the FBI, the Justice Department, and several summer project offices and movement lawyers. We expressed our concern about the lack of "law enforcement and lax protection given to the civil rights workers in Leake County, especially in the city of Carthage. Consistently, voter registration workers have been harassed and those guilty have not been apprehended or prosecuted." Summary of complaints:

> July 15—Two voter registration workers struck while canvassing. Attackers first spoke with police, who then walked away from the canvassers. Sheriff informed of incident, with description of men given. Men not apprehended.
>
> July 16—Minister with Summer Project struck while sitting in car. Incident reported, men not apprehended.
>
> July 18—Voter registration worker arrested for speeding (witnesses say she was traveling 40 mph) and charged with going 48 in a 45 mph zone. Released after dark and not provided police protection beyond city limits.
>
> July 18—Homes in Harmony community shot at. Reported—no investigation.
>
> July 23—Voter registration worker threatened by armed man while making phone call in public phone booth. Incident reported to police who did not respond at all. When worker asked for protection, response was: "If you came in unprotected, you can go home unprotected."

The letter closed, "If this pattern continues, we will be forced to seek federal protection. Order must be maintained."

WINSON HUDSON:

In the spring of 1964, Aaron Henry, our NAACP state president, told our local chapter about the plans for Freedom Summer, and we all went to Jackson and they told us what was happening and we decided we wanted some of the student workers to come and help us. We came back home and checked to see where the young people could stay, and after the training for them in Oxford, Ohio, we had thirteen come to Harmony—three black and ten whites, male and female. Because Headquarters was in Canton, Theodis Hewitt, married to Dovie's daughter, Jean, was the coordinator for the work, and I was the director of the summer project here. James Chaney stayed with us on and off and Michael Schwerner stayed with Dovie a while, before they was killed in June. Chaney and Theodis stayed in jail in Canton for a while and laughed about a big dog that was near them and would growl when they would move. Theodis stayed thirty-two days and Chaney might have got out a little bit ahead of him. Now, this is before they went to Oxford, Ohio, for the training.

When they came back from Oxford, we met in the Masonic Temple in Jackson. It is so big and you couldn't find standing space in there. We was driving down deciding how many would be there—they said it would be a thousand. So we had thirteen to come and we had 'em housed fine.

Around June 12, the students came rolling in. We were waiting on them on the old Harmony School campus, 'cause all of the buildings were still there and we had been cleaning 'em up. A big U-Haul load of books had been brought in and put in the old shop building. As soon as the students came, here come the sheriff and his deputies and asked them, "Who invited you all here?" I walked to the front and said, "We invited them here." The sheriff asked did we know we were on private property, and I told him how our parents had bought this land and Julius Rosenwald money helped us build these buildings. "It belongs to the County now," he said, and ordered the students to the courthouse to register and identify themselves. He ordered us to clear the buildings in three days. We moved the books to different houses and held our meetings under shade trees and at our homes.

I took two girls, Annie Pearl Clay and Pam Gerould, and Dovie took two girls, Jane Adams and Carole Grosse, and others took boys and girls. But, after staying here a while—I mean—it wasn't four or five days before people were flowing in here to check on their students and children. Those parents were senators and lawyers and doctors, and that relieved us, because the community was covered with white visitors and all kinds of cars coming in, looking for the Hudsons and looking for the McDonalds, because they'd know we was supposed to be head leaders of those kids. Those workers was plain cute. I mean, they didn't know nothing about washing dishes in a dishpan, and scalding 'em in dishpans. They didn't know nothing about our outdoor bathroom, and all that kind of stuff. And one time I found 'em washing their hands in the water bucket, where we had to drink water. And I said, "Look here, honey," I said, "you wash in the foot tub or the wash pan and dash it out. This is the water has to stay clean to drink." "Yes, Ma'am. Yes, Ma'am." So they were nice. They were very nice.

The students was teaching our young people literature, and having other classes, reading and writing, and they'd just get somewhere out under the shade trees up around the store. We were upset, because we didn't have nowhere to meet. That's when the people began to want somewhere to have meetings—a building under our own control. Cleo and Theodis suggested we build our own building, and those workers began to make contacts with their folks and friends to solicit money and we finally got it started. We bought a plot of land from Olen Dotson, and different money for lumber and the other materials and donations from people were coming in. Cleo had a big part in organizing this. He knew the man in Walnut Grove where they got the lumber from and went and talked with him, and the man told Cleo he would bring the lumber right out, and we started to build the frame. We started off with five dollars and others pitched in. In less than three weeks we had the Harmony Community Center.

When the summer workers came in here, we did get a lot of help—food and lots of books and whole big old vans of clothes come in. Then things got worse when the workers—Chaney, Schwerner, and Goodman—were murdered. Their bodies were found shortly before Debra Lewis was to go to the white school. They were found over in Neshoba County, our neighbor, about thirteen miles from here. The two counties are partners, 'cause we do a lot of our business over in Philadelphia, the county seat. We were so upset and sad about the murders, and word was out that Cleo better not go to Philadelphia, because he was likely to get killed. It was so much tension here because the Citizens' Council and the Klan and groups like that was active at that time. We couldn't tell where they were, because they were everywhere. You see, the Citizens' Council was the rich white folks—the bankers and the big folks. And we considered the Klan as poor and ignorant.

People who were keeping the Freedom Summer young people or working with them, had to be careful. Clyde and Hazel Harvey, two of our big supporters, got into trouble. One day, Hazel had gone to Carthage to register to vote, and the sheriff broke into their house and found some beer, and they put Clyde in jail for over three months. Hazel worked in Head Start for a long time, and it was real sad because some years later, she lost Clyde, and their son Eric, and their grandson Michael in a drowning accident.

No matter what the whites tried to do, we kept having meetings at my house and other places in Harmony. Benny Bounds and the group from Carthage came over here, because it was the only place where civil rights stuff was going on and sometimes people would come to look at us, like a circus or something and mostly to see what was going on with the white students they saw around here. People would run from you like you was something wild, and our Carthage people were afraid, because the black townpeople depended on white folks for a living.

By this time, we had also organized the Freedom Democratic Party, like the other counties where the workers stayed. They taught us how to hold a precinct election, and do the other things to make us official. Over to Ofahoma and Carthage, the black community participated with us, and we had our own district caucus. "Just go to the poll. Go to your voting place. If nobody's there, just nominate yourself as a delegate and bring us your material." We loaded a busload, and went down to Free Trade, our voting precinct, and when we got there, and went in the place for you to vote, the woman run us out. "Don't you come in here," and she was pretty mean—talking about guns, and they ran us out of the store. We had the county convention at Harmony Center, and didn't have many people come, but we got us a delegation, and me, and Dovie, and Choice Collier, another one of our leaders, and my husband went to Meridian to the district caucus, and then Cleo and Choice left there and went to Atlantic City to the Democratic Convention. I didn't go because I had all this going on with the students who were still here. There was a lot of tension, and I was afraid to leave the community, since the schools were going to open in a few weeks. But we helped get that busload of people to go to the National Democratic Convention in Atlantic City in August, with a few delegates from here, and you wouldn't believe what fools we were. When they got up there, we couldn't get nothing.

Then that whole time, we was testing public accommodations in Carthage. We knew the Civil Rights Act in 1964 said we could eat at places that didn't serve black people. Sometime we went to three or four places a day, and they would slip cards under the plate before they'd put our hamburger down, saying "The eyes of the Klan is watching you." But we would just go on and eat—me and Dovie and our brother Glover and L. V. Overstreet, and some others was always with us. One time at the Crest View hamburger place, a man told us to wait right there—that he was going to get the police. So we obliged and stayed there—didn't mind if we got arrested, but the man or police never did come back.

9. Crest View restaurant in Carthage, where Winson and other members of the Leake County NAACP held sit-ins during the 1960s, in protest of the restaurant's resistance to integration. Personal collection of Jewell Dassance.

So Freedom Summer brought good things. Later in the fall of 1964, the famous comedian, Dick Gregory, and Charles Evers, Medgar's brother, sponsored a big turkey thing. Dick Gregory brought two great big old vans—greaaaat big trucks, I don't know, long as this house here, full of turkeys, maybe 500 turkeys—and brought 'em to Jackson. We went in Behonor's truck and Cleo's brother, Joe C. Hudson, came too. We went early, and we notified the people that was coming in from Lena and around, watching us, you know, what we was doing at the community center. And the first night we went to meet Dick Gregory there in Jackson—he hadn't ever made it there with the turkeys. They called in and said the turkeys were still up north. We sat there all day until they said it'd be tomorrow. So we came back home, and got up the next day and went back down. We were about the first ones. A lot of people were afraid, but we brought back two big pickup loads of turkeys—just as much as we could pile up on there. And when we was coming on the first day, somebody trailed us. And so, when we went back the second day, we told Charles, "We might not make it back with these turkeys—we was trailed and pulled over once by the police in Carthage." And Charles said—you know, Charles wasn't nonviolent—"Get you a shotgun, and when they stop you, let 'em have it. If they mess with you, let 'em have it. It's time out for us petting these white folks—these crackers." Charles believed in taking care of yourself. He wasn't as easygoing as Medgar. We came on back the second day with the turkeys, and it was a big gathering at Harmony Community Center. People were there from Lena and Madden—done eased in that night waiting on a turkey. And you talk about a turkey thing—we had us a turkey thing. I had never had a big old butterball turkey. And people was coming in to get those turkeys and away they would go. They didn't want nobody to know they'd been there. Some who lived at Lena—they'd come in and get the turkeys and go way north and then switch around and come back to Lena. Some poor people we knew was afraid to come to the center, so Cleo took the turkeys to them in his truck. We had to give 'em all out, 'cause we couldn't do nothing with all them turkeys. And it made us have a real good Thanksgiving and a Christmas. We divided ours—couldn't use all of it for Thanksgiving, so Dick Gregory and Charles helped everyone have a turkey for Thanksgiving and Christmas too.

Freedom Summer made us excited about keeping the movement going, and in 1965, we heard from civil rights workers about the Head Start program for children. The federal government was going to pay all expenses for these programs. I couldn't believe it. First, I went to a training program in Mt. Beulah, Mississippi, on how to organize a Head Start program, and Minnie Lewis, Herbert Dotson, Diane Hudson, and Jimmie Dale Greer went with me. We came back to Leake County and got a committee to help start our program.

It was hard to get people interested because they were afraid. The community center had been bombed twice, hitting right up close to the building. That same night the men of Harmony shot the Klan truck all up. Harmony Head Start was the first center organized in 1965, and it was funded for six weeks and then the OEO [Office of Economic Opportunity] in Washington cut us off. We kept the center going for six more weeks with volunteers. People picked up the children in cars and brought them to the center, and brought cooked food from home to give them lunch. Sometimes, Behonor McDonald and Olen Dotson used their store to cook food. Some people laughed at us saying that we Head Start people didn't have enough education and what could we teach. The sad story was that the all-white school board wanted to take up all the money and take our children and organize their own Head Start program.

Our Head Start programs got funding in 1966, and I helped organize the Pilgrim Rest Center, Rising Chapel Center, Ealy Center, and Ofahoma Center. I started out as a teacher, and then was center director and then got promoted to countywide education coordinator. Later I worked as a social worker for Friends of the Children, after it wasn't CDGM (Child Development Group of Mississippi) any more. I went to New York City for training on how to work with children and it was a wonderful thing. One teacher gave us something in a foreign language and I didn't know how I was supposed to understand nothing. He was trying to show us that this is how grown people must seem to little children when we talk to them. Then I held workshops back at home for our staff, and people came from all over to see our Harmony center.

In 1966, Marilyn Lowen from New York, working with CDGM out of Jackson, came to visit us. She was our field trainer, and we traveled to the Head Start centers in other parts of the state. We always taught the teachers never to beat or hit a child—to talk to 'em—and we taught 'em songs—just no way of measuring how them programs made a whole new batch of black kids in Mississippi—made 'em not be so afraid, taught 'em to read and like books and how to make friends. One time in 1968, Marilyn was pregnant

10. Winson G. Hudson Head Start Center in Carthage, established in 1998. Personal collection of Chea Prince.

and we both wore the same red dress—kind of African style. We made them for workshops we were doing on Africa, and this was new for them kids.

In 1968, when I was working in Head Start, I had a staff car and my assistant, Dorothy Battle, was driving. We were down near Forest, Mississippi, and Dorothy tried to pass a big truck on the bridge and went head-on into the bridge. My niece Wardine Needham and her baby were visiting from Michigan and were with us—coming to my house to visit—and they came over from the back seat. Wardine's hip was out of place and skin was torn off my head. The baby and Dorothy were not hurt. The ambulance came from Forest and when I came to myself, blood was covering my face, but I refused to let them touch me. I had civil rights and voter registration materials in the trunk although we had been warned not to carry it in staff cars. I got my box of materials and handed it to my daughter, Annie Maude, who had come over from Decatur, and then I walked over and got on the stretcher. They carried me to the hospital in Forest and the doctor did a good job on sewing up my head. I was placed on the north end of the hospital and late in the night, I heard a lot of arguing. Someone was saying, "Bring her out from there." They brought me to the south end and all night I could hear a white man cursing. I didn't know what was going on. The next day a friend of mine eased in and said, "They brought you from the black part down here with the whites, because they said you were a freedom rider."

In a day or so, Marilyn Lowen came to visit. She told me that orders had been given "to make sure you and your niece get everything you need. They are afraid more freedom riders will come." Marilyn and I are good friends to this day and she helped me a lot with this book.

The Head Start in Harmony stayed at the community center for a long time, and we had some hard times. Couldn't get no local doctors to give medical care to those little children, and Dr. Robert Smith, Dr. Aaron Shirley, and Dr. James Anderson came from Jackson whenever they could, or we had to carry 'em out of the county. And then the program was getting too big in the eighties. We had eight units by then, and we needed air conditioning, central heat, and fireproof buildings, and we moved into some mobile buildings up on the hill where the Harmony School had been. Then later on in 1998 they opened that brick center down in Carthage and they named it after me. Head Start was another big program for us, because it gave us jobs, and especially for our little children, it opened up a whole new world. You know that children live what they learn.

In 1966, we also heard about the STAR (Systematic Training and Redevelopment) program coming through OEO (Office of Economic Opportunity) and the Department of Labor and going to Catholic parishes. Richard Polk, my neighbor down the road and NAACP member, worked so hard and got one here at a Catholic mission in a little community called St. Anne, with a school and all. I was on the local advisory board and that was a wonderful program. It taught people to read and write and trained 'em to get ready for jobs and to be part of the political process. And it was so integrated—training whites and blacks and Choctaws—but it made a lot of people mad. Richard was the director and he had a white teacher there and after about six months the whole mission got bombed—nothin' left. When Cleo and some of our men heard about the bombing they went to protect Richard's house in Harmony, layin' on top of cars with their shotguns, because we were afraid he might be next. Now that teacher at STAR had a little brother who heard some white men talking about the bombing and he named some names and that little boy got beaten so badly, had a ruptured spleen and died and nothin' ever done about it.

After that the program moved closer to Carthage and it did so much good, until the funding was stopped about four years later. We used to laugh with Richard Polk when he would tell us about hearing an explosion of any sort and his STAR staff saying, "Well, they missed us this time."

So Freedom Summer gave us lots of good things in Harmony—some for a short time and some that lasted. Our Harmony Community Center, Head Start, turkeys, STAR, knowing that some young white people cared, and lots of hope.

Chapter Five

"FIGHTING IS AN EVERYDAY THING": THE CONTINUING CRUSADE FOR CIVIL RIGHTS

After the drama and violence that often accompanied voter registration, desegregation of schools and public accommodations, and 1964 Freedom Summer activities, many black communities in Mississippi settled into quieter battles. Although the struggle became almost "a way of life" for African American leaders in local communities, it was often frustrating and discouraging. In spite of some gains in voter registration and school desegregation, life for the majority of black people was (and is) still desperately unequal. Luckily for Winson and the Harmony community, contacts with the "outside world" remained, and she continued to call upon the national FHA, Justice Department, NAACP, and the American Friends Service Committee for intervention and support. School problems continued, and from telephone service to roads, health care, land retention, housing, and voting, the late sixties, seventies, and eighties presented continuing challenges to Harmony.

Local newspaper articles from these years reveal the doggedness of the Leake County NAACP chapter, with Winson as president and a membership of seasoned and dedicated Harmony activists. Winson's main interest was health care, perhaps because she had suffered so many losses among her own family and friends.

As her friend and physician, Dr. Robert Smith from Jackson, put it: "Sometimes in the midst of rural poverty, the people don't realize their own condition or the condition of the people around them until an outsider comes along and points out the horrible environment. But in rural Mississippi during the 1950s and 1960s, the situation regarding the health of the people, black and white, was so visible that it was obvious something had to be done. Children were starving, mothers, themselves malnourished, were delivering children with severe health problems right from birth, and a lot of them didn't make it past infancy. Those who did often developed serious health problems early in life that were not treated and got worse until they died early or either had to live with a condition that might have been prevented with the right care. The health situation was that of a third world country."

The Carthage paper in September 1971 ran a story about Winson's testimony at the August meeting of the American Hospital Association in Chicago. "I'm from the red-dirt road country where the KKK watches over every move. There's not a single doctor in my county who will accept black Medicare or Medicaid patients, except the few they need to treat in order to get government money. We have more than

300 Head Start children in our county that we have to transport to other counties for medical treatment." One of the white doctors in Carthage responded that the "good people of Leake County" should be aware of "what this woman is saying about us when she goes north."

Successes in local school desegregation, voter registration, and health care, along with her NAACP and Democratic Party work, had indeed propelled Winson from local activist to state and national spokesperson for black Mississippians. At home, as her crusades continued on for decades, bringing increasing national prominence, and as her pronouncements received wide new coverage, she remained an anathema and enemy to most of the white community. She also encountered the continuing hostility of some blacks, even those who were beginning to reap the benefits won by early Harmony fighters.

In 1965, the year after Debra went to the school, they was going to take students in the twelfth grade and the second and third and then add more each year until the grades met. Dovie's daughter, Joan, went in as a senior and Carol Overstreet too. Carol was L. V. Overstreet's daughter and L. V. was always fighting along with us. Carol was real dark and Joan you couldn't tell from white—Joan had this red hair, just like them Barnetts. Joan and Carol was buddies, and they were treated really bad in the schools—name-calling and spitballs and shoving, and they didn't graduate. They had to go to Meridian and take some courses that summer in order to get their high school certificate. School people said they didn't have enough credit, but that was just an excuse, 'cause back then you just graduated. They didn't intend for 'em to graduate—just used an excuse to keep them from marching.

And even in the eighties we had problems with the school board. I was head of the NAACP and we would show 'em that the school was 51 percent black students and most of the teachers was white—and the teacher ratio was way off. And that Carthage High School, that big town school—until 1988, they didn't have a single black man there. They did not want black men working with their white students. Not a single black counselor even.

I had my two grandsons, Donovan and Kempton, staying with me. They finished at Edinburg here in the county. They had this white counselor, and he didn't do nothing. We had to go in and search and see what classes they needed, because they had been going to school in Texas and had missed some subjects. They were about to keep them from graduating, until we got in there. In Texas they were taking subjects like Spanish, and my grandboys can speak Spanish, but we didn't have a single foreign language in the county. So, when they got here, they were behind in some of their subjects. They had more than the children here, but they didn't have what they were supposed to have in Leake County. But we got it together, and they took these correspondence courses, and they finished all right. The principal of the school used to tell everybody to treat those boys right or Winson Hudson would be calling Washington, D.C.

We had to watch the school system all the time to make sure they were following the court orders. They made our black Jordan High into a junior high, and they even tried to move it once, and that's when our young lawyer friend, Mel Leventhal, came in and we forced them to bring it back. Mel came down every break he had from law school up North, and then he came down and worked at the Jackson office of that NAACP lawyer's group for seven years until 1974. Me and Dovie went to Jackson to see Mel, and we cried and cut up, and Mel said, "We'll get 'em back to court," and he made them bring that school back. They had closed Jordan High, and took it for a dump place over in there—breaking out the windows. Mel sued the school board. Me and Dovie carried that affidavit to the school board's lawyer, and he was so sick 'til he was almost in tears. He said, "I told them that they wasn't going to get by in moving that school." So we won and it came where they had to assign white kids to Jordan. But then the white kids started withdrawing to go to the private academy. Mel Leventhal laid with us to that day we got Jordan School back. We loved him. He made them do right about that school—clean it up and fix it up and watch over it.

But they were still firing black teachers for nothing and some black people going along with it. So we were still fighting. Even in 1989, when a black teacher dropped out somewhere, a white replaced them. We didn't have a single black in a supervisory position when we got federal Title I funds. They hired an assistant superintendent, not even announcing the job, and I said, "If the superintendent is white, the assistant superintendent should be black," but they paid no attention. We finally got straight with them on the school lunch problem and the children enjoyed that—black and white.

We even had a battle to get us telephones in Harmony. See in the fifties and sixties, we didn't have no telephones. All around us, north, south, east, and west, they had telephones but in this black community, we just couldn't get service. We tried and tried and we couldn't get 'em no way. Then our state NAACP president, Aaron Henry, called a state conference of the NAACP—it was 1967. He told us to come to Clarksdale where he lived, about 150 miles over in the Delta. So, with our old truck and cars, we didn't have nothing fitting to go in, and we got a friend named William Jackson who carried us around sometimes—and me and Cleo and Behonor McDonald got him to carry us in his new Dodge pickup. When we got up there at Clarksdale, we looked, and we saw white men standing around and walking outside the Holiday Inn where we were going to meet. We saw Klansmen riding by in their pickup trucks with all these guns up in racks. One of the black men with the NAACP came out and told us, "Lock your car doors, lock your pickup—somebody stay outside at all times. We're integrating the Holiday Inn today." And boy—1967, and man, there we was, way up in Clarksdale, got to go all the way back home from way up the Delta, integrating the Holiday Inn. "Turn the back of your car where the tag can't be seen so good." So we scuffled around to prepare, and William Jackson, part of the time, would stand back there and cover up the tags of his car so they couldn't see where they could trail us home. And those Klansmen, they were riding that road—Highway 61, past the Holiday Inn, coming in and out of the parking lot while we were trying to get into the conference room in front—kind of like a lounge. Way up in Clarksdale.

We sat around there and had our conference, and we discussed all kinds of problems we was having. And Miss Vera Pigee was very active—I believe she was the NAACP secretary at that time, because her and Aaron Henry was some of the main leaders there. Aaron had been locked up before and put on the Clarksdale garbage detail, refused to pay a fine so they'd put 'em out on the road chained together—Aaron Henry and about six or seven more. I don't remember the names, but I saw it on television and knew right then, I wanted him to be my leader. Him and Medgar Evers both—they made me strong!

Now at that meeting, Miss Pigee was complaining to the group about how many threats she was getting—somebody would hit on the telephone, and bump on it, boom boom on her telephone—and she said that they'd harassed her so until she was going to have her telephone took out or change the number or something. And then Behonor and Cleo was touching me and saying, "Tell 'em. You're the president. Tell 'em about the telephones in Leake County and how we can't even get 'em." So, when Miss Pigee got through telling her story about how she was being harassed by telephone, then one or two more said they was getting threatening telephone calls. I stood up and I said, "We don't even have a telephone in Harmony community." I said, "All around us—we're surrounded by whites, and we're in this all-black Harmony. We've tried all through the late fifties and sixties and on, and we haven't been able to get telephones. We have one black man on the outer edge of the community and we have used his telephone, but we can't use it any more. We have to go all the way to Carthage to Myrick's Funeral Home—closest one we can get—ten miles from Harmony community."

Then I told about how we do when danger comes. "Somebody's up watching all night, and whenever somebody comes through, a car that we don't know, then we have a sign. My husband or somebody'll shoot once or twice, or somebody'll get out and ride the roads, and blow a whistle so many times—long and a short, or three shorts maybe—to tell everything's all right. We didn't have a lot of cars coming through here because of the roads, but when a stranger came through, we know it."

So when I got through telling about the trouble in trying to get the telephone in Harmony, Gloster Current from the national NAACP office, director of branches across the country, was there, and Joe Rauh, the white labor lawyer from Washington who had helped us with the Freedom Democratic Party. Aaron got up and said, "Here's a woman would just be glad to have a telephone." So Gloster Current got up and said, "You mean to tell me that telephones are all around you and you can't get a telephone in the Harmony community?" I told how we had tried and tried—while the civil rights workers was here and other times, and we just could not get telephones. We hadn't thought about Gloster Current, or New York people, or about going through a whole lot of steps. Now I had sent a letter once to Gloster Current for black veterans who couldn't get on veteran disability, and we got three men on. One got $2,500 by just writing a few lines to Gloster Current, and told him about this man was totally disabled and he needed money. Then two over at Lena—one got $1,800 and the other one got $2,200 of back time.

So, back to the telephones. Gloster wrote me a letter on the Monday when he got back to New York and told me the name and address of the president of the telephone company in New York, and then he told me the president of the telephone company for Mississippi, in Jackson. And he said, "Mrs. Hudson, you will have telephones in three months' time." And boy, in three months' time those telephones was ringing plain everywhere in this community. We were just really proud, because we were on an eight-party line, but that was better than nothing. A lot of people don't know how they even got telephones, but this is the way we got 'em. When I learned the man's name in Jackson and made a complaint, got to know him well by phone. I never did see him, but I called him, every time collect, and he made them bring the phones here, and we were some glad people to get those telephones, because the Klan was really riding then, and they had bombed Dovie's house twice in less than three months. We knew they would rally in that field where highway 35 meets road 48—right at the turn-off to get to Harmony. So we needed those telephones. No more our men standing in the bushes beside the road, in gutters, and in ditches, having to guard this community.

After I learned about the man in Jackson, I didn't have to bother Gloster no more about telephones, because me and the supervisor in Jackson, we would communicate after we got the lines. Miss Marie Rogers wrote a letter to me one day—I didn't even know her—and she said, "Mrs. Hudson, I live in Marydale"—that's about eighteen miles northeast from here—Klan area back then, and she needed a phone bad. So I called Jackson and told about Miss Rogers—that she wanted a telephone. In a few days she called me back and said, "Miss Hudson, I thank you very much. They came out and they put me in a telephone." So the news started spreading around, and the next one was Miss Flossie Gray. She lived in the extreme western part of the county. She said, "All of these big white folk around here got phones, but they won't put me in no telephone." I called the supervisor at Jackson. I said, "Got another problem. Miss Flossie Gray in the Ofahoma community don't have a telephone, and whites all around her." He said, "How far is it from a house?" I said, "It's right by a house." He said, "All right. We'll get telephones out there."

And from then on, I didn't have no problems. And long as he was there—I heard he took up another job later on, and went to another state—but from then on, me and him would call. He'd call me or I could call him collect, and any problem that we had with telephones, he would see to getting things fixed. Sometimes a telephone, being new, they'd get out of fix, and I'd call him. I'd say, "Phone's acting up. We don't want no problems out of these telephones." And he'd send somebody right on in to fix 'em. So we worked that out.

Then, in 1967, I began to work with a group in Washington [Citizens Crusade Against Poverty], and they had heard about Harmony. A representative came down and toured the county with me looking for hungry people. I carried him to houses where little babies had starved to death. Folks were feeding them on powdered milk, and one little baby was so sick you couldn't hardly hear him cry. We went to some Indians' places where they were just eating bread and drinking water and sometimes commodity beans. Large stomachs and little bodies, little hands. We went to see some old people in the Lena area and asked them, "Do y'all get plenty to eat?" "Yes, sir, we got plenty. Look at the commodities stacked up there." And bugs was all in their commodities, and sometimes they'd just give them to the hogs.

So we looked at the commodities—peanut butter, meal, flour, and powdered milk—no value in it. And they were cooking on a wood heater that's made out of a drum, with a flat top, and the house was all smoked up. "Yes, sir, we get plenty to eat," they said, and after that visit I was called on to testify on hunger and starvation in Leake County in Jackson before the U.S. Commission on Civil Rights.

After we testified some times for the Crusade people—mothers starving, babies starving, and people everywhere talked about these things, they did a report, "Hunger U.S.A." It really opened some eyes and people like Robert Kennedy helped and that's when they did away with the commodities and brought in the food stamps. Then, I wish you could have seen people here, pushing a buggy in supermarkets after that. All kinds of food—string beans, cereal, something that they never had and milk and eggs. And that's why I pushed for the WIC program too—that's Women, Infants and Children—to help feed them. But the white folks in Carthage took over that WIC program under the welfare programs.

We raised a lot of sand about starvation and nutrition and I believe in Head Start, and they are all mixed in together—school issues is nutrition and nutrition is health and on and on, but my baby was that health care. I gave so much to that health care for the poor and community health centers, maybe because of the suffering that I have seen, starting with my own family—my own mother's death and my two sisters, and so many others dying from lack of health care. In the sixties, when we went to see a doctor, you'd sit in a segregated office, in a room closed off—sit all day and have to wait on the whites to get served first, or whenever they felt like waiting on you. My sister-in-law died for the lack of attention. A doctor was treating her for sugar diabetes, and when she died, she had cancer. I called her daughter in California and said, "Come home at once. Your momma is deathly sick." I carried them both to Dr. A. B. Britton, our good black doctor in Jackson, and he said, "Has anybody told you that your mother had cancer?" Said, "No." Said, "Well, she's got it in the last stage. There's nothing we can do for her." They put her in the hospital and she lived a little while. The white doctor had never done nothing—just opened her mouth. I don't know as he ever took a blood test. And she'd say, "Doctor says I'm getting along fine. I'm better," and she was going down day by day.

There were so many incidents like that—how black folks would go to that hospital in Carthage or to Emergency, and they'd just give 'em a shot and send 'em home, or send 'em to Jackson, with some dying on the way. It is unbelievable. And that's why I testified in Washington with this group from Watts, California, and Detroit, where those riots had been. Those people there was asking for five million dollars, and I said, "We don't have nothing. We don't have a black doctor, and we don't have a hospital that we can go to close by for good treatment. We have to travel seventy-five miles if it's an emergency—some dying on the way."

Now the hospital in Carthage was built with part Hill-Burton funds—that's federal money and meant that they couldn't discriminate, and we knew it. Dovie's husband, Arden, had died when all this Movement came on. You couldn't tell him from white, but when he was in the hospital, they had him down in the basement—him and two or three more blacks down in the basement—water dripping, brooms and mops and things. His doctor was kind of liberal at that time, and he came to see him and had a fit. They put Arden up on the floor where the other patients were. It's just a one-floor place with a basement. And so then they put the blacks on the south end of the hospital in what must have been a big waiting room—women on one side and men on the other—and then in one or two hospital rooms, they had this big curtain separating the hall between the blacks and the whites. My brother Frazier died in that hospital too.

Then one day, Reverend R. L. T. Smith, the black minister who worked for civil rights, from Jackson came and spoke to us at First Baptist Church. And he had a patient behind the curtain in the hospital and we told him, and Reverend Smith said, "That's just what I want to do—visit my patient. Let's go." Then we got our note pads—Reverend Smith and me and Dovie—and we went in the front of the hospital, and the first thing we did, we went and drank out of them white fountains—wasn't none back where the blacks was. Next thing we did, we went and used the bathrooms. Then we went to the north end where the white patients was in these nice rooms, and all these nice facilities back in there. Then, we was just walking and writing, and the whites was peeping out the door at us and the blacks too—they was peeping. But we felt big because Reverend Smith was with us. So Reverend Smith went down and seen his patient—went through the curtains and down to the black end of the hospital.

We looked, and we took a note of everything we saw. Reverend Smith said, "I'm going to get in touch with the Department of Justice tomorrow." He called on Monday morning. They gave the hospital seventy-two hours to desegregate or close down. So what they did, they moved the curtains. And they say they brought a black man off of the street, that was a caretaker for the yard and put him on a gown and put him in the bed in the white section. And actually, I'm sure we hurt a lot of people in the long run, because they singled things down to one bed to the room so there would not be no black and white together. We was better off when they could put lots of us in the waiting room. And there weren't black doctors 'cause they couldn't use the hospital.

So then folks started hearing about me and my work, and I got involved with some black doctors in Jackson who formed a group called Mississippi Health Care for the Poor. We believed we should have health centers where poor people could come. These doctors, Dr. Aaron Shirley, Dr. Robert Smith, Dr. James Anderson, and Dr. Charles Humphrey got me to travel to the American Hospital Association in Chicago in 1971 to testify about the lack of health care for poor people. Little me, no degree or nothing, and I made national headlines—helped get a big Hinds County Community Health Center, instead of operating in school buses. They sent me to Chicago, two years on the straight, to testify at the Association meeting along with all these doctors and health professionals from out West and Detroit and Chicago.

After those two meetings, Dr. Robert Smith brought me to Washington and we all demanded to meet with the president. Those radicals from out West wanted to organize a big march on the Nixon administration. That's when I raised sand, and told them that people were dying where I came from, and we had lost faith in this society. When I made national headlines again and got home, couldn't get nothing in the paper here that I wanted to say. The big to-do was, "stop this woman from going north, we must ignore this woman," and some even threatened to sue me to stop me from going to these meetings. See, I had testified also at Meharry Medical School in Nashville, Tennessee, about lack of health care for black people in Mississippi, and I had gone other places across the state talking about this terrible situation, and they just wanted to stop me from spreading the word about what all we needed for black and poor people.

When I got back from Washington, D.C., there was talk about a three-county health program in this area, and an assistant to Richard Nixon had told me to make no noise about it because they was going to have something going here in a few months, and they promised to notify me of what they was going to have. They went on to tell me I needed to get a place for a community health center. I couldn't hardly sleep at night, I was just so upset over what all needed to be done. So I communicated with Dr. Shirley from Jackson who hired my cousin to do a community survey, and we found Leake County was too small and that these other bigger places had Health Maintenance Organizations. I put all the money I had to buy three acres for a center on the outskirts of Carthage, and we had a little satellite center there, but we finally had to go in with Madison and Yazoo Counties, and Madison County already had a building, and they got the center. So now it's the Madison, Yazoo, and Leake Family Health Center in Canton, and it's for the poor—if you don't have no money, you don't pay no money.

So you see, fighting is an everyday thing—don't never rest. All along I had to harass them to make sure they kept doing right—just like the school system. That's all I can do—just raise a lot of sand. It was hard during the Reagan years. When Carter was in there, we had it made. I mean, we could do a lot of things, because I was on his advisory committee to tell about problems in Mississippi, and I have a photo of me with President Carter. So I lobbied in Washington a lot—even back to the Kennedys, walking those halls trying to see officials from Mississippi, like Representative Jamie Whitten, Senator Stennis, and Senator Eastland—they treated me with such hospitality. As long as I was up there testifying, I was a hit—just don't do it at home. And I would visit Representative Shirley Chisholm from New York and other black Congresspeople, and they always told

Best wishes to Mrs. Winson Hudson --
Jimmy Carter

11. As special assistant Louis Martin (center) looks on, Winson greets President Jimmy Carter in October 1978, on a visit to Washington. She was selected as one of three black leaders from southern states to have lunch with the president and discuss minority issues. Personal collection of Winson Hudson.

us that they represented us, even if our own elected people would not speak for what all we needed.

Then there was the battle over the roads in Harmony. In 1976, our NAACP chapter filed a letter of complaint with the Office of Revenue Sharing in Washington talking about "racial discrimination for not paving roads in the Harmony community, with it being all black." Forty years ago, these roads were so muddy when it rained, you just had to slop, slop, slop to try to get to the highway that came just to the edge of the community. Harmony is shaped like a circle and this highway 488 came to the edge and then it made a half circle and went way all around to the east side, when they could have come straight through. So when the county was going to get that revenue-sharing money, I wrote a letter to the Justice Department, and got the NAACP involved. I got to know the fellow at the Office of Revenue Sharing, in Atlanta, and they came out and made a survey. See, I was already mad because they had also built a road and brought it just about a mile down below me here and then they stopped it—just a little piece down before it got to me. I had already met with the supervisor, Crawley Alford, about the highway. He had been there twenty-five years, and he said, "You ain't going to get no highway. I ain't got no money to bring a highway." Then he told some others, "As long as Winson Hudson lives, I'll never bring a highway through there." That's when I wrote the Justice Department, Civil Rights Division, and they came out to do a survey. Now, the complaint was about the road that stopped before it got to my house, but when they came out and found that highway 488 had circled around Harmony community instead of coming straight through, they told the county, "This is the road that ought to have been put here, instead of going around through the white community."

Okay, when they finally brought a road, it came down by the Williams's store, but the supervisors still wasn't going to put no road near my house, as long as I lived. I laid real low for a while and then got some folks together to talk about the supervisor, Crawley Alford. Some of the black folks loved that man, but in all those twenty-five years, still couldn't get to their houses on those bad roads. Even after the federal people gave the supervisors so many months to put in a road, they just threw something down—a bad road and even whites had to travel it when the old bridge was out. Then we made a deal. There was a man running for supervisor against Crawley, and we asked him, "Okay, if we put you in, you're going to fix our senior citizens' building and you're going to bring a road through here?" He said, "I'll do the best I can, because if I get in I want to stay there." I said, "Okay. We're going to put you in, and we're going to look for you to treat us right." We got around to organize against Crawley, and some of Crawley's white friends tried to get him to come to fix it with me and promise me a road through here. And he still said, "Before I stoop, I'll lose. I'll lose the election." So we decided we'd work to get the whole five board of supervisors out. We went to the other parts of the county, and whites and some of the blacks would say, "Let one or two stay on." And we'd say, "No, let's get the whole crowd out." And, for the first time in I don't know how many years, we wiped it clean, and we got this other supervisor, Jack Jones, and he started bringing this road through here. We got the best road of anybody, because by then, the state was getting community development funds and the highway through here became a state project instead of a county road program. But this road right in front of my house is called "Hudson Road," and I am proud of that sign they put up in 1992. So everything was a long fight.

Now Crawley Alford did help us get the Senior Citizens' Center. We got $12,000 from the county and went to work on the old shop building—all that was left of the Harmony School, up on the hill. The county said we could keep it for twenty years and then it went back to them. We got it fixed up good, and we all enjoyed it for a long time. It was air-conditioned, carpet on the floor—small, but we could meet up there and talk about things that we couldn't argue about in church. We raised money for heat and planned programs and let people use the baseball diamond out there.

There were always so many small things right here, local problems—like a lady who would come and was about to lose her house. And I let her have $400 to make payment, or rather I gave her a check for the $400 cash she gave me, 'cause they wouldn't take cash, and she had like thirty minutes to get it there. Saving our people's land and houses has always been so important, and when I worked with the Emergency Land Fund, I couldn't count the number that we was able to save. We would just get on that FHA and keep having 'em investigated. It's not much problem to get a home if you got a job and can pay for it. I hate to see people with no place to live, and can't get a house. So you pressure the FHA, so that any black person who qualifies can get a loan. If you go over Harmony and compare things with forty years ago, you wouldn't know it. All kind of beautiful homes. Now, the Veteran's Administration has built some homes too, but in 1960, there was not a single brick home

12. Winson standing at the junction of Galilee and Hudson roads. The former was the original name of the town of Harmony, while the latter was named for the Hudson family property in Harmony. Personal collection of Jewell Dassance.

around here from FHA money. We kept hearing about the FHA and what they could do for you. Even heard it on the news. Then you'd go in the office and pick up materials and you'd see all these flyers saying what could be done, but when we applied, we were told we didn't qualify. We kept working away.

So, it's been a long hard fight for so many things, and my husband, and my friend Behonor McDonald, and some others, just fell dead, and one of these days, I'll do just that. But I'd rather have that kind of death than to suffer. My husband was under so much pressure, and Behonor too until it just finally got 'em. Cleo fell dead in 1971, saying, "I'm tired, and we're going to have to stop." The last words he said—"I'm tired. I'm tired. I told you, I am tired." He was talking real good. And I said, "Okay. Okay." So I've just been going on for the years since. I had some friends that offered me to come to New York, and I thought about it. My daughter was in Texas, her and her boys, and I said, "I don't know what I'll do." And I thought about it and thought and then I said, "No, I ain't going nowhere, I'm going to get back out there."

And I did, and got things together, and I went into the cow business—became a businesswoman. We already had cows—Cleo did, but he wouldn't sell them, so I went and sold off all of the old, poor cows—culled 'em out and sold 'em off. Then I turned around and bought purebred, and I started growing cows. I mean, I got good money out of ones that I sold off, and then I turned and bought cheap, cheap cows, and I did that until I retired in the 1980s from Head Start work. It was hard going out and about and then come

13. Winson's house, on Hudson Road in Harmony.

home and see after the cows—come home at night in the cold and go out and throw hay. I got Dovie's boys to come down and throw out the hay sometimes, and cows are not like dogs and things—just throw the hay across in the wintertime and fertilize your pasture in the summertime, and they make their own living. But I just got tired, and I sold them off—sold all my cows. But I liked that farming—I liked them cows. That helped support me so I could do my community work and go around the country and keep doing work for freedom.

Chapter Six

"THE COST TO BE FREE": REFLECTIONS ON A LIFE OF ACTIVISM

During my visits to Harmony, Winson and I sat in her living room, where she would muse about the past and the present. Or we would get out and ride around and she would point out places where certain things happened in her story. We passed the Crest View Dairy Bar in Carthage, where blacks were refused service and now are welcomed. She showed me the Barnett Mansion in Standing Pine and talked again about the absurdity of race and color when Barnett and Hudson and Choctaw blood were all mixed somewhere along the line.

And among the funniest happenings—on two occasions—going with Winson and family members to the Hitching Rail Restaurant in Carthage, and when Winson came in, Carla, one of the white waitresses, literally hollered, "Here comes Ms. NAACP," and rushed up and hugged her, and she then received royal treatment from everyone. But mostly she talked about her concerns for the future, and whether the young people will continue the fight. The theme of the land is always on her mind and she recalls her work as county contact for the Emer-

gency Land Fund, which started in the 1970s and still exists today to help retain black-owned land through legal, technical, and financial support. Winson knows intuitively and historically that losing the land in the Harmony community is a threat to the independence and cohesiveness that has been part of their heritage for over 100 years.

Winson is concerned about the materialism among young people of today and that their goals are so self-oriented rather than directed toward benefiting the total community. She continued to tell me more stories and mentioned all the other good people who helped and what all she has left out, but she stopped when she realized that she wants to see this book done—and soon. Her humor is still evident. She was showing me all her nice Christmas presents when I was down in December 2001, and commented, "They must think I am about to go," and she laughed.

I have a house full of plaques and citations and honors and awards, but the most exciting thing that ever happened to me was being in that book with Dovie, back in 1989. It was called, *I Dream A World: Portraits of Black Women That Changed America.* That's the most publicized thing that I've ever had. The book was by Brian Lanker, the photographer, and he came here and he stayed part of a day and we set up at Dovie's. She was kind of sick at that time, and that's where he did the interview and took the photos of us. Then they set up this exhibit at that big museum [Corcoran Gallery of Art] in Washington, and we were invited to the celebration and could bring a companion. Well, Dovie wasn't able to go, and they gave me and my daughter the trip. I got to see Oprah Winfrey, and Alice Walker and her daughter, Rebecca—I hadn't seen her since she was a baby. I won't never be able to tell enough about that Washington thing. I was on crutches and I was in a wheelchair, and when they called my name to go up on the stage, I left my wheelchair, got on those crutches, and I was up there as quick as any of the rest of 'em. Then they rolled me around in the wheelchair, which made it very, very comfortable. I didn't worry about getting tired, and my daughter was there to care for me. And that Brian Lanker is a wonderful man and we had all this staff from U.S. West, and the Kodak Company. I talked to both of those big men, owned those big corporations. And I told them I want them to do something for Harmony. "And I want you to get some help for Harmony so that I can leave something here for the people to remember." I still want a building up on the hill where our school was, so I can have a space in there to put up my plaques, and all this I got that tells the story of Harmony—a place where we can hold conferences for young people to try and hold Harmony together after I'm gone.

I'm teaching these youngsters, like my grandsons, Donovan and Kempton, and all these young adult mothers and fathers, to hold to this land. I care a lot about the land. I love it, and there won't be no more land. That's why I worked so hard with groups trying to save black folks' land. "Hold Onto the Land" was the motto. There will be people, buildings, and cars and things going to the moon, and people living on another planet, but there won't be no more land, 'cause once you lose it—that's the end of it. So we

14. Winson receives the Distinguished Service Award for Outstanding Community Service from Mississippi Governor William Winter, April 1983. Personal collection of Winson Hudson.

need to arouse young people's knowledge of how valuable this land is here and how it's always been important for black people—since slavery. We depended on this land for a living, and young folks need to cherish it like we did and still do.

But a lot of young people think that having a job is the answer to everything. They say, "Yeah, I'm working at Sonic's," or "I'm working at Ward's," and "I'm working at McDonald's or the Casino." Now, those girls are running those cash registers, running places to eat, and we got plenty of our folks are working in the courthouse, and some still don't support us at all. And I tell 'em, "You know what? Do you know how you got here?" "Yes ma'am, and I am proud of it," they say, and they don't know you couldn't even eat in front in a restaurant, much less work there—except in the kitchen. I say, "Do you know the pressure and the hardship that we had to go through to get you jobs or into the courthouse?" 'Cause, you see, even now, before we get behind anybody to vote for, they have to promise to hire black people. If they don't, we don't support 'em.

Some older people, now in their fifties and sixties, who left Harmony, still think enough of the land to hold on to it and after a while maybe some of 'em will find that they have to return to it and become interested in it. Already a lot of our people who went away are moving back from the cities. This is home. Once you get old, you want to go back where you used to eat and breathe. Like my baby brother Osly. He lives in Portland, Oregon, but he loves to come home. Comes and stays and just flops around—uses my car—goes to see the trails he used to walk and the little branches where the fish used to run. When he comes out, the frown's left his face and he's just relaxed—says he feels like a different person when he comes back now. He used to love to

15. Winson holding photo of Dovie and herself that appeared in Brian Lanker's book, *I Dream A World: Portraits of Black Women Who Changed America.* Hudson is shown here in 1989, at the debut of Lanker's exhibit at the Cocoran Gallery in Washington, DC. Personal collection of Winson Hudson.

find clippings about me and Dovie and admired us for the stands we took. But it was in all of us, passed on from my father, but it was just too dangerous for the men sometimes.

Back in the late sixties, when people from away began to come back for funerals and things, we began to talk about a time to get folks back to Harmony the same time every year. And Harmony folks from Chicago were talking about it too—wanting to come home to see what was happening. We held a planning meeting at Christine Warren's Beauty College and decided to set the Saturday before the second Sunday in August for our "Homecoming." In the early seventies we had a fish fry and then, the State Department of Agriculture said they would cook for us and set up big cooking places for chicken and fish. But they stopped when others started asking and they couldn't do it for everyone. But it still grows every year and one time, we had almost 2,000 people coming home from California, New York, Florida, and Chicago, and lots from Jackson. In 1996 at the Harmony Homecoming, Congressman Bennie Thompson brought Congresswoman Maxine Waters from California, as a surprise, and she told us she had been all over the world and nation and had never seen anything like Harmony—she is a powerful woman. My niece, Allean Gates Leflore, lived in Maxine Waters's district out there before she moved back here in 1992. But that was a great homecoming, lots of people and just like every year, I got them to sing our Harmony School song:

Harmony, we love you, we'll ever be true,
We'll stick to you whatever you may do.
Harmony, our colors are purple and gold,
We'll surely be gold wherever we stroll.
We'll keep you on our minds and never stray away,

You know we love, for you'll always hear us say:
Oh Harmony, we love you.

Everybody coming back, and the singing and all—it means so much to all of us who have stayed.

I wish I could find some young people with the same energy and concerns that would just take up the struggle and carry on. Sometimes they seem so lost, and I know times have changed but there's still a lot of work to be done. What they got on their mind is a good job and a car, good house, and "educating my children." Should be thinking about educating "our" children—not just thinking about themselves. I worry what's going to happen to this younger generation—the things they don't know. We've got some black lawyers and black politicians and that's good, but some of those people are very selfish too—fighting among each other.

The other thing black people, young and old, need to realize is how they are putting so many of our young men away into prisons. If you are black and poor, you can't get no bail money and you can't hire good lawyers to keep you from going or get you out. Something that happened really broke my heart, and I can still cry about it. In 1987 they executed Edward Earl Johnson at Parchman State Penitentiary in the Delta. He was one of my Head Start children I had recruited from Walnut Grove, and he was the sweetest little boy and didn't ever give us no problems. His Grandpa would bring him every day and then would stay to help out in the Center. Edward Earl was accused of killing a Walnut Grove night marshal in 1979. They say he was trying to break into a white lady's house. He was only eighteen and had just graduated from high school. We think he signed a confession after the police told him he would get treated better if he just signed it. I went to see him a lot when he was at Parchman, and when I asked him if he did it, all he would say was "They said I did." I remember the newspaper saying that sentencing Edward Earl to the gas chamber was the first death sentence handed out here since 1916, when they hanged my uncle Alonzo. They killed Edward Earl at midnight, and that night we was all down at the True Light Church in Walnut Grove, praying and crying and praying. I wish you could have heard us at midnight when they said he was dead.

I took a reporter from the Jackson paper to see his mother and grandmother right after that to tell about how quick the whole thing went—seven years when sometimes all those appeals can take 20 years or so. And I have done my best to help black people on this going to jail and no justice in the courts. Until my health got bad, I was down at the jail and courts a lot, and, sometimes my just being there helped get better and fairer treatment for our people.

But I'm not sorry about a thing, and I have so many good memories of the places I've been and people I've met. One time in 1991, I went to the University of Virginia to talk in Julian Bond's class. I had met Julian a long time ago—seems like he was just a young boy, and I would see him at NAACP conventions. Maxwell Kennedy, Robert Kennedy's son, was up there in Virginia too, and I met him. We loved them Kennedys, and we were so sad when they were gone. Seemed like they wanted to help black people. I was always active in the Democratic Party—it got integrated here after the fight by the Mississippi Freedom Democratic Party in the sixties, and I went all over for the party.

Now, Mae Bertha Carter, my friend from Drew, up in the Delta, was in Virginia too, to speak with me in the class, and Max Kennedy come to see us first at Connie Curry's place. Mae Bertha and I went to the back room and then

16. Civil rights leader Julian Bond and Winson, University of Virginia, 1991. Personal collection of Constance Curry.

came out. Max was sitting on the couch, and we sang a song for him. It was about Abraham and Martin and John being killed, and everybody being gone and we sang about them and then we sang:

> Has anyone here seen my old friend Bobby—
> Can you tell me where he's gone?
> I thought I saw him walkin' up over the hill,
> With Abraham, Martin, and John.

And Julian Bond came in the house and we was all crying.

And you know it's funny, lots of our people now is sorry that they didn't get out there themselves back then. Even some of the teachers called us old cows—"walk around here like old cows, and half dressed, and they ought to go somewhere and try to get some clothes." And some of those teachers that talked about us, they wish now that they had been a part of it—that they had sent their child to school like Debra. I never was a hostile kind of person—to get mad and raise a lot of sand about the people that tried to do us in—white and black. Just take what I had and go on. Some black folks went to the white people and talked about us and then they turned out to be our best friends. But back in the early days, you didn't have no friends. It was a lonely walk.

Today, when they call my name in church—I'm proud. I just feel good because for the first time in my life, just the last few years, here on the local level I've got a lot of certificates and plaques and tributes and dinners, and I'm proud of it all.

17. Winson (l) joins Jean Fairfax (center), Barbara Moffett, and Mae Bertha Carter (r) at a November 1990 American Friends Service Committee meeting on civil rights workers. Winson and Carter (a civil rights activist from Sunflower County, Mississippi) were featured speakers. Courtesy the American Friends Service Committee.

So, I mostly feel happy—joy most of the time about my work over all the years. That's my life. Only thing is I wish I could see better and didn't have to walk on crutches. I wake up every morning and that's when I get on my mind what I'm going to do, or what can I do today—write a letter to somebody. You stay here a little while and you'll find out that it's somebody all the time in trouble. I felt bad for a long while when I saw new people coming in and changing so many things we had worked so hard for and not respecting me—saying I should step aside. I just wonder what's going to happen. People know that we're not progressing enough, but they don't say nothing. But I prayed on it and it's okay. Time passes on.

So I just try to tell the story about what happened and is still happening and I pray and hope. That poem I wrote back in 1989 says it all—about the "cost to be free."

EPILOGUE

Constance Curry

Leake County is growing. The 2000 census shows that the population of 17,000 in 1970 has increased to 21,000. This includes 12,000 white, 8,000 black, 1,000 American Indian, and 500 Latino or other. The Chamber of Commerce attributes this in part to Choctaw Maid Farms, Inc., the enormous poultry processing facility on Highway 35 North, just outside Carthage. It is open twenty-four hours a day, five days a week. When I first saw it one evening, I thought the brightly lit 315,000-square-foot building, situated on 100 acres, was one of the casinos springing up in the area on Choctaw land. The company was founded in Carthage in 1948, as the R & R Hatchery and Milling Co., and operated a feed mill and delivered feed to poultry and livestock producers in the area. Now, the Carthage plant employs over 2,500 people—15 percent Hispanic, 65 percent black, and 20 percent white workers who process 25 million birds per week.

The opportunities created by the diligence of the Mississippi Band of Choctaw Indians in and around Leake County also account for part of the population growth. Beginning in 1830, under the U.S. government's removal policy, approximately 18,000 Choctaws were forced to move to Oklahoma. The Choctaws in the present-day Band are descendants of those who refused to leave their homeland. Instead, they stayed, hiding out in the forests and swamps, barely surviving, sometimes sharecropping for oppressive white landowners. In 1918, following a deadly flu epidemic, only about 1,000 Mississippi Choctaws remained in the state. As Winson points out in her story, the plight of the Choctaws was often worse than that of black people. There were varying amounts of support for the Band from the federal government during the first part of the twentieth century, but change for the better began in 1959, when Philip Martin, a young Choctaw, who had been a representative on the Mississippi Choctaw Tribal Council, was chosen as chairman. There were strong parallels over the years between Choctaws and African Americans in Leake County in their resistance to oppression and the struggles for land retention, economic opportunity, better education, and political power. However, with Chief Martin's leadership, the patterns of poverty and repression began to change. Today, the reservation land encompasses more than 25,000 acres with a population of more than 8,300 Choctaws. The casinos, manufacturing, retail, and commercial services operated by the Band in Neshoba County created some 5,200 jobs. Over 3,000 are held by non-Indians. In many ways, with jobs, excellent schools, and their own government, the Band has made more progress than their black allies from former days.

The opening of the Walnut Grove Youth Correctional Facility in March 2001 has also created jobs for Leake County residents—97 percent of the 200 employees are local, 59 percent are black and 53 percent are women, and there is wide gender and racial diversity in administration, security, and education units. A conversation with Warden

Douglas Sproat reveals some interesting facts about this facility. It is part of the burgeoning privatization of prisons seen throughout the country, but the state awarded this contract to a Mississippi firm called Tuscolameta, Inc. Tuscolameta is the name of the creek behind the facility. It is a $48 million building set on 100 acres of land, air-conditioned and state of the art. There is a capacity of 976 beds, 500 of which are occupied by youth between the ages of 13 and 20. Forty of 500 are serving life sentences. Eighty percent of the inmates are black. Warden Sproat has made sure that the facility offers treatment and mental health programs, and vocational and academic training.

Finally, as Winson says in her reflections on Harmony today, black people who left some time ago are coming back home. The crime rate is low, economic opportunities are growing for the moment—the unemployment rate in Leake County dropped from 12.9 percent in 1986 to 5.6 percent in 2001. The rural county, with its rolling hills, is only fifty miles from Jackson.

Positive changes have occurred in the political arena, thanks to the hard work and arduous days of voter registration and getting black people to vote, as described in Winson's stories. A Leake County Voters' League now works with the NAACP chapter and there are ten black elected officials. Ruby Graham is the first black woman elected judge of the Justice Court, Western District, and Pamela J. Carson is the first black woman elected circuit clerk. There is one black state representative from Leake County, one black on the Board of Aldermen, two serve on the County Supervisors

Board, two serve on the Board of Education, and two serve on the county Election Commission. Although the voting rolls are no longer kept by race, a present-day estimate of black registered voters is 35 percent.

Mary Gates is now the chair of the Leake County NAACP chapter. She reminded me of Winson's role in bringing her back to teach in Leake County, after the school board had fired her in the sixties for associating with the NAACP. We talked about the changes, setbacks, and successes in the present and of the NAACP's continuing struggle. Like many rural communities, and in spite of growth patterns, a plethora of social evils are eating away at the future. The teenage pregnancy rate is one in four, and there is a 38 percent school dropout rate. Unemployment is always looming and illegal drugs are peddled to unsuspecting youth. The NAACP has had several complaints about discrimination in the criminal justice system and at the Regional Correctional facility in Carthage.

There are public schools at Carthage, Walnut Grove, Edinburg, and Thomastown with over 3,170 students enrolled and three private schools with an enrollment of about 800—predominantly white. Leake Academy, a private school that first operated in 1964 in a church basement, in response to public school integration, is still in operation. Their enrollment of 500 is predominantly white with some Native Americans, Asians, and Indians. There are no black students there at this time.

Although the student population in the public schools is predominantly black, school administrators and teachers and counselors remain predominantly white, approximately

70 percent, and the black community wishes, in particular, that there were more black counselors.

During my time of working on the book, several people from Winson's past have come with me to visit with her in Harmony. In May 2001, Mel Leventhal and Mary Norris came for a weekend. Mel, now practicing law in New York City, was the young lawyer with the NAACP Legal Defense and Education Fund in Jackson who, with great determination, had helped the Harmony community in their many early disputes with the school system. He had not seen Winson in over thirty years. Winson's entire face lit up whenever Mel walked into the room that weekend. Mary Norris, from Philadelphia, Pennsylvania, long associated with the American Friends Service Committee, had transcribed all of the original interviews with Winson, taped by Jean Fairfax in 1989. Mary had not seen Winson in several years, and she teased Winson about knowing her story as well as she did. Winson also allowed Mary and me to go through her voluminous papers and boxes and try to sort them and file them—an enormous act of trust, according to her friends and relatives. On that visit, we took Winson and her daughter, Annie Maude, and her niece, Joan Griffin, to stay one night at the Silver Star Casino Hotel in Philadelphia, Mississippi. We met other relatives who worked at the casino, and some of us played the slot machines, while all enjoyed the wonderful inexpensive buffets, and watching what may be the most integrated and convivial gathering of people in the state.

On a July 2001 visit to Harmony, I met Jean Fairfax and Derrick Bell at the Jackson airport, and we drove to Harmony for a tribute to Winson, sponsored by the Leake County Branch NAACP. The Carthage Econo-Lodge was filled, and we happily made reservations to stay at The Silver Star Casino Hotel. Derrick and Jean wanted to see the flourishing community and activity on the Choctaw reservation in Neshoba County. Drive thirty minutes from Harmony through rural Leake County, enter Neshoba County, and there looming on the horizon is the Silver Star Hotel and Casino on the right, and the enormous Golden Moon Hotel and Casino under construction on the left. What a shock for people involved in the sixties civil rights movement in Mississippi to see this enterprise in Neshoba County. Our main association with that county is the place where the three workers, Chaney, Schwerner, and Goodman, had been murdered in 1964, their bodies hidden in clay banks and not found for two months.

The Appreciation Program that Derrick, Jean, and I attended on Sunday afternoon, July 22, 2001, summed up Winson's work in an amazing way. Held in the community meeting room of the Carthage Bank Annex, it included tributes from family, friends, and leaders, past and present. Mary Gates, current NAACP president, and Richard Polk, long-time friend and community worker, recalled Winson's devotion to adult education, the local NAACP, and the progress that had been made in the thirty-eight years she served as president. Jean Fairfax and Derrick Bell spoke of the days they first met Dovie and Winson and their families and worked with them the summer of 1964 to send first-grader Debra Lewis to the white school. Democratic Congressman Bennie Thompson, himself a civil rights worker from the sixties, and Mississippi House Representative Bennett Malone spoke of how Winson "keeps them in line" on political issues. Mr. Malone, who is white, and other politicians have realized over the years that Winson and the NAACP can make or break their re-election possibilities. Mississippi House Representative Ferr Smith also honored Winson's work. A long and successful road led him to serve as the first black elected to the Leake County Board of Supervisors in the eighties, and in 1992 to the state legislature. This is the Mr. Smith, who, as a young college student in 1962, wrote to Robert Kennedy protesting the use of literacy tests, which had barred his father from voting in Leake County.

Before the celebration, Jean and Derrick and I went to a stone memorial marker in Carthage that reads:

> "Lone Negro Girl,
> You shaped the course of history in Leake County.
> Child of the Civil Rights Movement,
> From labor to reward. We love you!"

Debra Lewis Wilson died on February 4, 2001. She was forty-three. A street in Carthage was named after her, and a memorial celebration was held on Sunday, February 25, 2001, at the First Baptist Church in Carthage.

One continuing source of pride for Winson is the large brick building on Highway 16 in Carthage where the Head Start program serves 171 children from all over the county. Opened in 1998, it is named the Winson G. Hudson Center for Families and Children, and is part of the statewide Friends of Children of Mississippi, still funded by the federal government. The center serves white, black, Choctaw, and Hispanic children, and they have a translator on staff. The modern facility reflects the progress since Head Start began at the small Harmony Community Center built by summer volunteers in 1964, when parents were afraid to send their children because of several bombing attempts. The remains of the community center and its Head Start activities are seen only in the broken, paint-chipped little horses and rusted slide on the weed-overgrown playground. The S. O. Williams Store, which stood next to the center and which served the community as a gathering place for eighty years and particularly during Freedom Summer, closed in 1999.

Winson and her daughter, Annie Maude, live in a brick house on Hudson Road, built in 1979 with the help of an FHA loan, which came through easily after the long struggles with the FHA in the sixties. Grandsons Donovan and Kempton Horton, both of whom have stayed in Mississippi, are frequent visitors and a great source of joy for Winson. Donovan, the oldest, born in 1966, lives in Jackson with his wife, Dionne, three-year-old son Ryan and ten-month-old daughter Tyler. Donovan graduated from Tougaloo, has an M.S.W. from Jackson State University, and is now a crisis intervention specialist with Catholic Charities. Dionne is a registered respiratory therapist with the University of Mississippi Medical Center. Kempton Horton, born in 1968, lives in Starkville with his wife, Lisa, and three-year-old daughter Lauren. Kempton graduated from Alcorn State University, is with the Office of Mississippi State Auditors, and Lisa is an assistant professor at Mississippi State University. Both Donovan and Kempton lived with Winson in Harmony during their formative years and say that she insisted on their getting a good education. They understand and appreciate the history and work of their grandmother and are determined to carry it on.

18. Winson's grandsons Donovan (r) and Kempton, December 2001. Personal collection of Constance Curry.

19. Winson Hudson in her home, 2000. Personal collection of Chea Prince.

The last time I visited Winson, in December 2001, we were going through some boxes of papers, and she found her favorite hymn. She asked me to read it to her and sang along in her strong voice:

> Once to every man and nation, comes the moment to decide.
> In the strife of truth with falsehood for the good or evil side.
> Some great cause, God's new messiah, offering each the bloom or blight,
> Parts the goats upon the left hand, and the sheep upon the right.
> And the choice goes by forever twixt that darkness and that light.

Winson thought for a moment and said, "They will sing it when they bury me."

INDEX